A CIP catalogue record for this title is available from the British Library.

ISBN 978 1 78629 041 0 (Paperback)
ISBN 978 1 78629 042 7 (Hardback)
ISBN 978 1 78629 043 4 (E-Book)

www.austinmacauley.com

First Published (2016)
Austin Macauley Publishers Ltd.
25 Canada Square
Canary Wharf
London
E14 5LB

About the Author

Born and raised in Karachi, Pakistan, Niloufer's love for food combined with extensive world travel from a young age inspired her to experiment with world cuisines. Niloufer gave her first cooking class to a group of school girls at the age of 17; loving the opportunity to meet new people who share her passion for food, she has gone on to give many, many more cooking classes in Dubai, UK, and Canada – where she has lived for the past 15 years with her family.

In 2013, Niloufer decided to start a recipe blog Niloufer's Kitchen where she loves to share old and new culinary creations to a following of 100,000 from around the world. Author of 10 e-cookbooks, she also writes for the Huffington Post, assorted magazines and journals from around the world.

You can visit her blog at www.NiloufersKitchen.com, and
follow her on Twitter @NiloufersKtchn and
on Facebook at www.facebook.com/NiloufersKitchen.

Niloufer Mavalvala

The Art of Parsi Cooking
reviving an ancient cuisine

AUSTIN MACAULEY
PUBLISHERS LTD.

Photo Credit to

Sheriar Hirjikaka

maplenama@yahoo.com

Book Cover credit to

Zara Contractor

www.zaracontractor.com

Dedication

Blessed are all whose parents support their passion in life.

To my dad, my light and life, snatched away in a second, yet left behind a legacy that continues with admiration few can dream off. He taught me kindness, generosity of mind and soul, acceptance of different capacities in mankind.

Passing on his love for travel, a positive zest for life and the mantra that family comes first; all of which has served me well.

The more I recall our daily conversations I can only be thankful for the years I spent with him. We were close in life and are closer in spirit. I continue to celebrate his short life; 2016 marks 25 years of his death anniversary. I am dedicating this cookbook to his infinite love for good food. His joie de vivre and love of entertaining everyone who came into his life continues to bring a smile to my face.

It is with an abundance of affection and pride that I write this memorial for my beloved father, Dr. Jamshed Hormuzshaw Wania. A product of BVS, he went on to study at Dow Medical College where he made many lifelong friends. Later travelling to the UK and USA to specialise in eye surgery, he earned his place both at the prestigious Moorfield's Eye Hospital London and Johns Hopkins Baltimore.

My parents Shireen and Jamshed Wania circa 1987

Generous of heart and mind, he strongly believed in sharing his wealth of knowledge as best as he could. He lived principally to be of service. He set aside each Saturday of his life toward treating the unfortunate who could not afford a specialist. He helped set up two major eye hospitals and led many eye camps, all of which were free. He trained young doctors in his clinic without compensation or hesitation in teaching them to be the best they could be. He had a heart of gold and never judged or discriminated. In death, he donated his corneas that served a young man well.

Dad had good values and morals in all he did, he taught my brother and me well. He loved people and never hesitated to chat with anyone. He loved to travel and had done so extensively with his adoring wife, Shireen. We lived in an open house and there was hardly a day in our lives when we had no visitors walk through. He always told us to greet each one with kindness and respect. No one ever left our home without sharing a meal or a cup of tea.

His better half, my mother Shireen, has been the yin to his yang. Exactly the opposite in nature, she is timid, shy and never raises her voice. Yet she was the pillar to our lives as she supported all his prolific ideas and lived his dreams hand-in-hand. She encouraged us to do our best and strive to reach for the stars.

My mum Shireen in her own right is an outstanding chef who only believes in perfection! She ran a successful cake business after the sudden death of my father. A perfect hostess, she loved to entertain and always created different menus for every dinner party she ever had. She went to the extent of keeping a log-book of what she prepared for her guests each time, so as to try and not repeat a menu! Art and music is her passion and the creativity of her cakes also overflowed to her talent at painting. She is the epitome of elegance. It is with her infinite knowledge and nurturing that I am able to do what I do best.

My Dad and I

viii

Another important person in my life has been my amazing paternal aunt, Villie. She has been my inspiration. Sharing our passion for food, teaching and experimenting with new ingredients, she has helped me in so many ways. I shall hope to keep her influences very much alive with the publication of this cookbook. I can only offer her my deep gratitude and affection. Thank you, Villie Fui, for always being there for me to lean on.

To my wonderful hubby and children, I could not have done any of this without you. To my adoring brother you are the reason I started cooking. To my other mum and dad, you both are the most wonderful in-laws anyone could ever ask for and I love you dearly. To all my friends and family, thank you for your loyal support and professing to enjoy my cooking! A special thanks to my friend, Sheriar Hirjikaka for his tireless and priceless contribution of beautiful photographs which have helped make this dream a reality.

Finally, here's a toast to my cookbook: May you be a Best Seller, bringing the joy and happiness of good food to the homes of each person you enter, just like you have brought to mine. Salamati!

My gorgeous aunt
Villie Mehta

The Art of Parsi Cooking

reviving an ancient cuisine By Niloufer Mavalvala

Originating from what was once the Persian Empire, Parsis are the followers of Prophet Zarathushtra, born in Airyana Vaeja in the foothills of what is now Central Asia.

Revealed over 3500 years ago, Zoroastrianism was one of the first monotheistic religions known to mankind. In spite of it being so old, it is a living religion for just under 200,000 Parsis (Indo-Iranian ethnicity) who have now settled and practice their faith around the world. It is unclear how many other ethnicities are practicing the faith.

The term Parsi, meaning from Pars (Iran) refers to those Zoroastrians who fled Persia and migrated to India between the 8th and 10th century. They landed on the shores of Sanjan, Gujarat where they were accepted on the strict condition of no conversion and hence began a new chapter for themselves.

Parsi cooking was to be shaped by history. Culled from two ancient cultures – Persia, from where we hail, and India, where we then settled – this unusual historical background gives Parsi foods a distinct and unique flavour. Recipes with dry nuts and fruits giving Shirini (sweet) flavours come from Persia, while those made with ginger, garlic, chillies and spices are Indian influenced.

Centuries-old ingredients like saffron, jaggery, cider vinegar, ginger, cinnamon and turmeric, all part-and-parcel of Parsi cooking, have been revealed for their great health benefits. There is much excitement to revive this ancient and unique Manna and carry forward traditions in the years to come!

Meat and eggs are two favourites of Parsi food; and garlic, ginger, onion and tomato make up the base of most recipes. While a range of spices, including cinnamon, turmeric, cumin, and chillies create the flavour, adding jaggery and vinegar gives a finishing touch. Tikhu-Khatu-Mithu (Spicy-Sour-Sweet) is considered the Holy Trinity of Parsi cooking, and perfecting its balance is the key between mediocrity and perfection in any Parsi dish.

A few of the quintessential names associated with the Parsi cookery repertoire are: Dhansak – a much-loved lentil and meat dish, the King of all foods Parsi. Add then Akuri and "Parsi Omelette" to the various assorted "per edu" (as in topped with an egg) dishes; this could be almost any vegetable like okra, potatoes, coriander, tomatoes, spinach, etc.

And of course, a true Parsi never forgets about his dessert trolley. Dessert is a definite "must" for Parsis. The delicious array of Parsi desserts, many of which use almonds and other nuts, are often enhanced with rosewater, cardamom, nutmeg, and sometimes a hint of vanilla.

The grandeur of the Lagan nu custard (custard pudding included in a wedding feast), the duo of Sev and Mithu Dahi (sweet vermicelli and home-made yogurt), and the Malido (a rich semolina based dessert originally made by priests' wives) are all irreplaceable old-time favourites. The various taffy-like sweets called "Pak" prepared by our grandmothers, have taken on a sudden interest and being revived with gusto. These include the Khopra Pak (coconut), Badām Pak (almond) and Eda Pak (egg), as well as the Vesanu, a complex mixture of seeds, nuts, ginger and other spices – this is often given to lactating mothers to renew their strength and energy after having given birth.

Mango ice-cream and Kulfi (ice-cream made with rich, evaporated milk) are an adopted part of the cuisine. Amusingly, the French caramel custard has long been considered a part of food without even adapting that recipe! I grew up in a family where we had caramel custard prepared fresh every day, until my father passed away. His family of seven brothers and sisters not only knew how to prepare it but also insisted each made the perfect one!

Teatime treats to dunk into a strong cup of tea are also essential. Included in this cookbook are Batasas, a savoury butter biscuit; Nankhatai, a sweet semolina biscuit; Kumas, a traditional saffron and yogurt cake topped with almonds and pistachios; and, Chaapat, a coconut-milk pancake with all the traditional Parsi flavours.

Other delicious sweet-snacks include Daar ni pori, a sweet lentil-filled piecrust; Khajoor ni ghari, dates and almonds in a semolina crust; Khaman na Ladoo, sweet coconut balls; and Bhakra, a deep fried semolina and saffron treat.

Pickles and Achars are the sidekick to most Parsi meals. Gharab nu achar, fish roe cooked in spices; Gajar mewa nu achar, carrot and dry fruit; and Buffena whole ripe mangoes stewed and cooked in spices, are just a few of my favourites.

Emphasis on seasonal foods for health and healing is an essential part of this ancient cuisine. It is commonplace for Parsi families to have home remedies, like turmeric with honey for infections, or preparing tea with fresh ginger, cinnamon and whole spices for a bad cold.

Recipes are not to be used as perfect, exact tools, but rather guidelines resting in our kitchens to be balanced and steered toward our taste buds. The spice, the salt, the sweet, and the sour in our dishes can be fine-tuned and perfectly set-up for our family and friends, only through our personal kitchens. The love and affection with which a dish is made makes it even more perfect.

Contents

03 **APPETIZERS – PEHLI VANI – FIRST COURSE**

04. Akuri (Scrambled Eggs with Spices)
06. Chicken Botis (Chicken Wings)
08. Tumtumta Jhinga (Prawns in spices)
10. Calamari Pakora (Calamari Puffs)

13 **SIDE DISH – BEEJI VANI – SECOND COURSE**

14. Papayta per Edu (Eggs on Potatoes)
16. Bheeda per Edu (Eggs on Okra)
18. Tamota per Edu (Eggs on Tomatoes)
20. Patra ni Machi (Fish with Green Chutney in Banana Leaves)
23. Masala na Khekra (Spicy Crabs)
26. Faraj (French Beans)
28. Paapri (Field/Sheet Beans)

31 **MAIN DISH – TEEJI VANI – THIRD COURSE**

RICE DISHES – CHAWAL NU BHONU

32. Marghi na Curry Chawal (Chicken Curry with Vegetable Palau)
36. Machi no Palau (Fish Palau)
39. Machi no Sās Khichri (Lentil-rice and Fish in Tomato Gravy)
44. Jhinga na Curry Chawal (Shrimp Coconut Curry and Rice)
47. Dhun Dar ne Jhinga no Pātiyo (Lentils with Rice and Prawn Chutney)
50. Jhinga no Palau (Prawn Biryani)
53. Dhansak (Lentils and Meat with Brown Rice)

58 ROTLI DISHES – ROTLI NU BHONU

59. Roast Gosh (Sunday Lamb Roast)

62. Papeta ma gosh for Ghambars (Potato and Meat)

65. Sali Marghi (Chicken and Potato Straws)

68. Chicken Badami (Chicken Almond and Yogurt Curry)

71 DESSERTS – MITHOO MŌNU

72. Parsi Lagan nu Custard (Parsi Wedding Custard)

74. Doodh Pāk (Almond and Rice Pudding)

76. Mango Ice Cream

78. Parsi Kulfi (Burnt Milk Ice-cream with Pistachio and Almond)

80. Ravo (Semolina and Egg Pudding)

83 TEA TIME SNACKS – CHAI NI SATHEH

84. Parsi Choi (Tea)

86. Batasa (Parsi Butter Biscuit)

89. Kumas (Parsi Cake)

92. Khatai (Parsi Sweet Biscuits)

95. Chaapat (Parsi Sweet Pancakes)

98. Malido

101 PARSI COOK'S SPICE ISLAND

103. Garam Masala – A blend of spices

About Dhansak Masala

106. The Ancient Art of Grinding Spices

Appetizers
Pehli Vani

04. Akuri (Scrambled Eggs with Spices)

06. Chicken Botis (Chicken Wings)

08. Tumtumta Jhinga (Prawns in Spices)

10. Calamari Pakora (Calamari Puffs)

Akuri served with crisp bread, butter and homemade jam.

4

Akuri - Scrambled Eggs with Spices

Sunday brunches and picnics are the happy memories associated with eating Akuri. Traditionally eaten for leisurely Sunday morning breakfast, it remains a favourite way of devouring eggs for most Parsis. Serve it with fresh crisp bread or toast, butter, jam and a pot of freshly brewed Parsi Choi (tea made with mint and fresh lemon grass blades).

Every family seems to have their own version of it. I personally prefer my family recipe, less ingredients with a great taste.

6 to 8 servings

- **4 tbsp oil**
- **8 green chillies finely chopped**
- **3 cups finely chopped fresh coriander**
- **3 large skinned, finely chopped tomatoes**

- **1-cup of finely chopped fried onion**
- **1 tsp salt**
- **16 eggs, room temperature**
- **Optional ingredient:**
  A dash of milk

In a skillet heat the oil. Add the vegetables and salt. Sauté it for 7 minutes while stirring on a medium flame. Cover and lower the heat, allowing the mixture to gently simmer until it is cooked through and the liquid has evaporated. This should take about 20 minutes.

In a bowl beat together the eggs with a dash of milk.

Pour the eggs over the cooked vegetables and keep stirring it constantly on a low flame until it resembles scrambled eggs.

Tips

Keep all the ingredients at room temperature to cook evenly and quickly. Use a food processor to chop the vegetables. Use only the pulse button to keep the vegetables from becoming one big mush.

Chicken Botis
Chicken Wings

Chicken Botis - Chicken Wings

These delicious, soft and creamy pieces of BBQ or grilled chicken can be served on skewers with fresh onions, tomatoes and a wedge of lemon. Boti-style, chicken wings is my take on Parsi-Fusion pub-grub; it's food to impress your guests, prepared in your own kitchen! Serve with yogurt raita or green chutney, lime, onions, cucumber and lettuce, pita or naan.

6 to 8 servings

- 1 kg/2.2 lb skinless chicken wings or chicken breast, cubed.
- 1-cup plain yogurt
- 1 flat tsp garam masala
- 3 tsp red chili powder
- 1/4 tsp turmeric
- 1 tsp cumin powder
- Juice from 1 lemon or lime

- 1 tbsp oil
- 4 garlic cloves minced
- 2 tbsp ground ginger
- 1/2 tsp salt
- Pinch of sugar
- A generous pinch of crushed saffron

Wash and pat dry 1 kg/2.2 lb skinless chicken wings or chicken breast, cubed. Sprinkle with salt.

In a bowl, mix to make the marinade: the yogurt, garam masala, red chili, turmeric and cumin powders. Also add the juice of lemon or lime, oil, garlic, ginger, salt, sugar and saffron threads.

Marinate the chicken overnight in the above mixture.

Preheat the broiler to 200 C / 375 F and cook for 10 minutes turning once, until golden brown. You may need extra time for bone-in chicken wings.

Tips

- Choose either wings without skin or chicken breast cut into small cubes. Bring to room temperature before cooking.
- If using bamboo skewers, presoak them in water for an hour or more to avoid them from burning.
- If cooking in an oven, spread the chicken out over a large baking tray, ensuring the pieces do not overlap.
- Use only thick yogurt. Other types of yogurt tend to release more liquid making it harder to grill perfectly.
- You can also BBQ the chicken but be sure to check the chicken is cooked through.

Tumtumta Jhinga
Spicy Prawns

Tumtumta Jhinga – Spicy Prawns

The literal translation of Tumtumta is delicious, mouth-watering spicy. This recipe is simple to make, with just a few ingredients. It is an ancient family treasure being revived for the next generation. The flavour really depends on the freshness of the prawns and spices. It is specially appreciated by prawn-lovers, who enjoy eating pure seafood – what we Parsis refer to as naki maal!

6 to 8 servings

- **1.5 kg / 3.5 lb fresh prawns, peeled, deveined and washed**
- **1 whole pod of fresh peeled garlic**
- **1 tsp red chilli powder**
- **1 tbsp cumin powder**
- **2 tbsp coriander powder**
- **1 ½ tsp salt**
- **Tiny pinch of sugar**
- **Oil as necessary to help combine the spices**
- **2 tsp red chilli flakes**
- **You also need:**
  - Rapeseed or sunflower oil to fry
  - 2 fresh lemons or lime

Grind together fresh peeled garlic, the red chilli powder, cumin and coriander powders, salt and sugar. Add the oil as necessary to help combine the spices; finally add the chilli flakes and give it a quick mix with a spoon.

Marinate the prawns with the ground mixture and refrigerate for a few hours or up to 24 hours.

Bring the prawns to room temperature before cooking. When ready to cook, heat a large skillet and add a tad of oil to "wet" the pan.

Pan-fry the prawns in 3 batches.

Keep the pan hot, flash-frying the prawns for a couple of minutes on each side. Squeeze fresh lemon or lime all over. Serve immediately with toothpicks.

Tips

- Do not overcrowd the pan.
- Each piece must touch the bottom of the pan.
- Wipe the pan with a paper towel between each batch if there is burnt masala residue left behind. This will ensure your next batch to be just as perfect as the first.
- Remember to bring the prawns to room temperature before cooking. Chilled prawns do not cook evenly and can end up being rubbery in texture.
- Use any size of prawns you desire. The cooking time will be dependent on the size. But the general rule of thumb is 3-5 minutes per batch.
- Do not use pre-cooked prawns for this recipe.
- 2 tsp red chilli flakes approximately equals 6 large dry red chillies.

Calamari Pakoras with Green Chutney and Sweet Red Chilli Sauce

Calamari Pakoras - Fried Calamari and Spices

Parsis have borrowed Pakoras from their Indian hosts. Crisply fried, it is a snack-food traditionally made with onions, potatoes and green chillies, served with tamarind and date chutney to dunk in. It is also associated with rainy days and a hot cup of tea!

The Calamari Pakora is a personal favourite and a new addition. As the culinary world gets more daring it seems nothing is out of bounds. Let's call this one Parsi-fusion. Serve these crisp freshly fried Calamari Pakoras with a traditional chutney sauce or any dipping sauce you prefer.

6 to 8 servings

- 6 calamari tubes
- 1/2 tsp salt
- 1/2 tsp garam masala
- 1/4 tsp cumin powder
- A fresh scraping of nutmeg
- 1 tsp red chilli flakes

- 1 tbsp finely chopped coriander leaves
- Juice of 1 large fresh lemon or lime
- 1-cup potato flour
- 1 tsp red chilli powder
- 1/2 tsp salt
- 3 cups of oil

Wash and evenly cut the calamari tubes in equal rounds, pat dry or drain well.

Toss the cut calamari with salt, garam masala, cumin powder, nutmeg and chilli flakes.

Then add the coriander leaves and squeeze the juice of the fresh lemon or lime.

Cover, refrigerate and keep up to 4 hours. Remove calamari from the fridge 15 minutes prior to frying.

In a bowl mix together the potato flour, chilli powder and salt.

When ready to cook and serve,

Heat the oil in a deep wok to a temperature of 180 C/350 F.

You can check if it is hot enough by dropping a piece of bread into the hot oil; if it bubbles and comes up to the surface the oil is ready to start cooking in.

Now add 1/6th of the marinated calamari into the potato flour. Toss it well and drop each ring into the hot oil. Work quickly. With a slotted spoon remove the rings and place on an absorbent kitchen paper. Repeat until all pieces are fried.

Serve this fresh and hot with an assortment of dipping sauces like blue cheese mayonnaise, sweet and sour tamarind chutney, harissa and honey mayonnaise or a sweet and sour chili sauce.

- There is a difference between squid and calamari. Calamari is softer and easier to cook. Calamari is smaller than squid, where the fins go all the way down. Like every other seafood try to buy it fresh from your fishmonger and not the frozen ones available on freezer shelves.

- The crispness will depend on the correct temperature of the oil. Over-heated oil will burn it while cooler oil will leave it soggy and greasy. Adjust the flame according to how quickly you can work. If it takes you sometime between the lots, lower the flame and then bring it up again. This has to be cooked on a high flame. It takes just one minute for each batch.

- Start by adding a few at a time. Your wok may be smaller or larger, so make sure there is at least 6 inches of oil.

- You may use gram flour/besan instead of the potato starch. But potato flour is lighter and cooks more evenly. If using gram flour, slightly lower the flame after you reach the correct temperature required, as it takes longer to cook through.

Side Dish

Beeji Vani

14. Papayta per Edu
    (Eggs on Potatoes)

16. Bheeda per edu (Eggs on Okra)

18. Tamota per edu (Eggs on Tomatoes)

20. Patra ni Machi (Fish with Green
    Chutney in Banana Leaves)

23. Masala na Khekra (Spicy Crabs)

26. Faraj (French Beans)

28. Paapri (Sheet/Field Beans)

Papayta per Edu
Eggs on Potatoes

Papayta per Edu — Eggs on Potatoes

I like to think of this as a quick fix dish. It blends the protein and vegetable combination in the best possible way. It is a comfort food that the family will enjoy any time of the day or night. Traditionally papayta per edu is served with a spicy carrot and dry fruit pickle (Gajar mewa nu achar) and fresh rotli or crisp bread.

6 to 8 servings

- **3 tbsp oil**
- **500 gm /1.1 lb onions, thinly sliced**
- **1 kg/2.2 lb potatoes, peeled and thinly sliced**
- **4 fresh green chillies, finely chopped**
- **1 tsp salt**
- **6-8 eggs, at room temperature**

In a large skillet heat the oil; add and cook the onions to a light golden colour.

Add the potatoes, green chillies and sprinkle with salt.

Keep the flame on a low heat. Cover the pan and cook through, until the potatoes are soft.

Add the eggs, cover and cook for 5 minutes or to your liking.

Tips

- If potatoes are prepared ahead it is important to heat them thoroughly before adding the eggs.
- Eggs must be at room temperature.
- You can use the slicer in the food processor to save time if you wish. It does both the onions and the potatoes, and you throw the green chillies in there too!

Bheeda per Edu
Eggs on Okra

16

Bheeda per Edu — Eggs on Okra

Growing up, we often had this simple yet elegant dish as a side. It was generally served with fresh rotli or crusty bread and the gajar mewa nu achar (carrot and dry fruit pickle).

On one of my cooking trips to Guildford, Surrey I was invited to teach a menu typical to any Zoroastrian-Parsi home. My class was a brilliant group of professors and teachers from the local university in Guildford. I decided to start the demonstration off with this particular recipe.

I had been reprimanded over my choice of menu at home and for choosing this dish in particular, but I decided to go ahead anyway — having already picked and prepared ahead of time for the occasion. Imagine my joy when the class voted this dish to be the most unusual and yet the simplest to make. It is with that in mind I share the same with you to enjoy.

6 to 8 servings

- **3 tbsp oil**
- **2 large onions finely chopped**
- **3/4th tsp salt**

- **1 kg /2.2 lb okra (ladyfingers), washed, tops discarded and slice**
- **A pinch of sugar**
- **8 eggs, at room temperature**

In a large skillet, heat the oil. Add the onions and fry until light golden brown. Add the okra to the onions, and sprinkle with the salt and sugar. Mix well and cook on a medium heat, shaking the pan rather than stirring, often. Cook until the okra is soft, about 30 minutes.

Before serving, heat the okra thoroughly; spread them evenly across the bottom of the pan. Make 6 wells with the back of a spoon. Break the eggs in the wells and sprinkle each one with salt and pepper. Cover the pan and lower the heat. Cook until eggs are set to your liking.

Serve immediately.

Tips

- Pick medium thin and crisp okra. They should be green without any black spots.
- Cover the pan and leave it on a low flame if you are busy working on something else.
- To avoid it being slimy, wash with cold water, chop the okra when cold.
- Avoid using a metal spoon while cooking.
- Ensuring the onions and pan are both hot before you add them in.
- Gently shake the pan to mix as this avoids breaking the vegetable.
- Serve this with a tomato, lime and ginger chutney and fresh warm rotli or crisp bread.

Tamota per edu
Eggs on Tomatoes

Tamota per Edu – Eggs on Tomatoes

Parsis have an infinite love for eggs. We eat eggs with most vegetables and in all shapes and forms. Here is a recipe, similar to thick tomato chutney, made in a style typically revering to the Parsi Cooking Trinity of Tikhu-Khatu-Mithu (Spicy-Sour-Sweet).

It is generally served as the second course followed by the Marghi na curry chawal (Chicken Curry and Vegetable Palau).

6 to 8 servings

- 3 tbsp sunflower oil
- 3 large onions, finely chopped
- 1 tsp garlic paste
- 1 tsp ginger paste
- 1 tsp ground cumin
- 3 green chillies, finely chopped
- ½ tsp red chilli powder

- 1 tsp salt
- 1 kg/2.2 lb tomatoes skinned and finely chopped
- 50 gm/2 oz jaggery
- 6-8 eggs, a room temperature
- 2 tbsp milk
- ½ tsp salt

In a skillet, heat the oil and fry the finely chopped onions until golden brown.

Add the garlic and ginger paste, the cumin and green chillies, chilli powder and salt.

Mix well and cook for 2 minutes.

Now add the tomatoes; be sure to add all the juices too. Also add the jaggery.

Cover with a lid on a low flame until mixture becomes thick, resembling "chutney" like texture. It should not have any liquid remaining in the pan. This process takes up to an hour.

Just before serving, reheat the tomato to a boiling point. Beat 6-8 eggs until light with 2 tablespoons of milk and a pinch of salt. Pour over the hot tomato mixture; turn the flame to low and cover the pan, waiting for the egg to set, about 5-7 minutes. Serve immediately with warm rotli or crisp bread.

Tips

- There will be a beautiful shiny glaze over the tomato mixture once it is done.
- Make this in individual portion ramekin dishes if you prefer. Top each one with a whole egg. Bake it in a hot oven or poach and place in each one.
- For best results, use ripe fresh tomatoes, preferably ripened on the vine.
- Scrape the jaggery before adding it to help melt it faster.

Patri ni Machi
Fish in Banana Leaves
with Green Chutney

20

Patra Ni Machi — Fish in Banana Leaves with Green Chutney

It has become a recent tradition associated with Parsi cooking to boast of its speciality of fish in banana leaves.

Being a blend of two cuisines, Indian and Persian, the tikhi (spicy) green coconut chutney and the use of banana leaves to cook in, is adopted and adapted from India. Blending the chutney to be Khati-Mithi (sour-sweet) is from our Persian roots.

Perfection in all Parsi Food is dependent on the fine balance of spicy, sweet and sour – tikhu khatu nay mithu. Long live this marriage of flavours!

Growing up in Karachi, we generally served whole White Pomfret fish – slit from one side and filled with green chutney, salted and oiled from outside and baked whole. Alternately thick fillets of white fish, like Surmai (king fish) and Ramas/Rawas were covered in green chutney and wrapped up in pieces of fresh banana leaf and stringed. Deep fried in oil just before serving, these freshly prepared pieces of fish were unfolded at your plate where the server ceremoniously cut off the strings with a scissor and the discarded leaf whisked away! It is not practical anymore to be able to cook, nor serve in that manner and so I share with you a simpler yet effective way!

Most of the fish mentioned above is available in your local Asian Super Market. Test for freshness by ensuring the colour under the gill is a fresh bright pomegranate or garnet red.

In my opinion, the fish fillets work best, although in India it is still a piece of Pomfret, served bone in, which is where all the flavour is!

6 to 8 servings

- **1-cup desiccated coconut**
- **6 green chillies**
- **½ tsp salt**
- **1 ½ cups of coriander leaves; packed tightly**
- **10 fresh mint leaves**
- **2 green peeled mangoes**
- **2 tbsp jaggery**
- **¼ cup fresh lemon juice**
- **1 ½ kg /1 ¾ lb white fish; cut into 10-12 pieces**

The Green Chutney

In an electric grinder/food processor or blender grind until fine and smooth the desiccated coconut. Then add the rest of the ingredients in order green chillies, salt, coriander leaves, mint leaves, diced mangoes, jaggery and lemon juice. Taste for the salt, the heat from the chillies, the sourness and the sweetness. Balance must be perfect.

The Fish

Wash and pat dry the fish.

Lightly salt each piece of fish before applying the Green Chutney.

21

Preparing and Assembly

On a baking tray lay out banana leaves, which have been washed, wiped dry and lightly salted. Brush oil lightly on the leaves and place the pieces of fish on it without overlapping any of them.

Top each piece of fish with green chutney. Gently press it down with the palm of your hands or the back of a spoon from end to end of each piece. Now cover the fish with more banana leaves that have been "oiled" on the side that touches the fish.

Bake for 22 minutes in a preheated oven at 175 C/350 F. Check to ensure all the fish is cooked through.

Discard the top leaves and serve on a platter with banana leaves.

Tips

- Fresh banana leaves are found in most countries in Asia and most Asian food stores across North America now carry frozen sheets for easy use. Simply defrost, wash and wipe them before using. It is definitely worth the extra effort.
- Desiccated coconut is available in most Indian stores as are all of the above ingredients.
- Traditionally thick fleshed white fish works best for this dish. Salmon, Tilapia, Haddock and Halibut fillets are some examples of what I use. However, each can be substituted for any favourite fish of choice.
- Green mango is a term used to refer to raw mangoes which are hard. Always remember to peel them before use, discarding the seed in the center.

Masala Na Khekra
Pan-Fried Crabs with
Spices

Masala Na Khekra — Pan-Fried Crabs with Spices

Crabs are found on the very bed of the sea, sunk deep down in the mud. They can be very small like the soft shell crabs or fairly large like the Dungeness Crabs; found in the waters off Coastal British Columbia. The other common variety is the Mud crab. Singapore is world famous for the Chili Crab prepared with these.

The Crabs must be very fresh when you buy them. They are generally sold 'alive' and cleaned on the spot for you. Wash them well with water and drain before you marinate them with the spices. Keep them marinated for a few hours at the most. They are best cooked on a high flame and eaten immediately.

Crabs are meaty and delicious. The best ones have an almost natural sweetness of the ocean, hard to describe. Growing up in Karachi on the Arabian Sea we often went out on hired trawlers for an evening out 'crabbing' with friends. The fresh sea breeze powering the sailboats while we inhaled the freshly cooked crabs prepared by the crew on-board seems like another lifetime! Sailing around the inner creek all evening totally dependent on the wind was an exhilarating experience. Often sharing stories and adventures with us we were often told by these "men at sea" that the crabs caught on moonless nights tend to be meatier.

6 to 8 servings

- 2 kg / 4.4 lb crabs, quartered
- 2 tsp red chilli flakes
- 1 tsp red chilli powder
- ½ tsp turmeric
- 1 ½ tsp salt
- 4 cloves of freshly crushed garlic
- Oil
- Handful of curry leaves
- 2 green chillies, slit
- 1 whole red dry chilli
- 2 fresh lemons or limes, to be freshly squeezed

Wash the crabs and drain them. Sprinkle all the dry spices over them; red chilli flakes and red chilli powder, turmeric, and salt. Toss them well and add the crushed garlic and a drizzle of oil. Toss again. Mix it well until the spices are spread evenly. Leave aside for at least an hour to marinate.

In a large skillet heat a dash of oil. Add the crab pieces, cooking them on a high heat for 3 to 5 minutes. Turn the crabs over and add curry leaves, green chillies, and dry red chilli. Cover the pan for 3 minutes. Give the pan a shake. Open and sprinkle the fresh lemon juice all over the crabs. Cover and let it rest for 3 to 5 minutes.

Serve and eat immediately.

- Do not overcook the crabs; they will feel like cotton wool.
- It is important to close the lid and cook for a few minutes as well as allowing it to rest. This 'steams' the crabs and infuses all the flavours well.
- Let the crabs rest for 3 minutes with the lid on to allow the juices to flow.
- If the crabs themselves are plump and sweet they need minimal of spices.
- Optionally, add a teaspoon each of grated fresh ginger and coriander, cumin powders if desired.

Faraj
French Beans

Faraj – French Beans

Naturally sweet, Faraj or French Beans are very easy to prepare. Cut at an angle and cooked with simple ingredients such as tomatoes and onions, it is often served as a vegetable dish alongside any main or even with scrambled eggs and fresh rotli, which makes for a complete yet simple meal. I often recall the joy of eating them freshly picked at a family friend's farm in Quetta, where we spent some of our summer holidays growing up. The crisp fresh taste of eating them raw off the bush lingers in my mouth to this day!

6 to 8 servings

- **3 tbsp oil**
- **1-cup finely chopped onions**
- **1½ tsp ground garlic**
- **½ tsp crushed cumin powder**
- **2 green chillies, slit whole**
- **1 flat tsp salt**

- **A pinch of sugar**
- **3 large tomatoes, skinned and chopped**
- **1 kg/2.2 lb French beans, cleaned and cut at an angle**
- **Optional Ingredients:**
  1 potato, diced in small cubes
  1-cup of green peas
  2 tablespoons of freshly cut coriander

In a pan heat the oil. Add and sauté the onions until light golden brown. Add in and fry for a minute, garlic, cumin powder, green chillies, salt, sugar, tomatoes and finally the freshly cut French beans. Sauté these ingredients for 5 minutes, cover the pan and let it cook in its own juices for about 30 minutes.

Optionally:

Add potatoes and/or green peas 15 minutes into cooking time. Add the coriander after ingredients are cooked through.

Remove from heat and serve with rotli or crisp bread.

Tips

- If you are using a packet of frozen green beans cut french style, stir fry the beans on a high flame first until all the water has evaporated. Do not add watery beans into the pot or it will turn mushy.

27

Paapri and a melange
of vegetables

Paapri – Parsi Style Field or Sheet Bean

A seasonal Indian vegetable, Paapri can be delicious if cooked properly. Not a popular dish with younger folk it needs to be spiced up and cooked with lots of trimmings, as shown in the recipe below. Although I grew up eating this regularly, it was not until I started cooking it myself that I actually started enjoying this dish!

Fairly popular in my cooking classes, it is a colourful array of vegetables all cooked in one pot. Paapri is a wonderful choice for a buffet table. Best served from the flat deep skillet used to cook it in!

6 to 8 servings

- **1 kg/2.2 lb flat Paapri beans, strings on side removed and washed**
- **2 onions, chopped (raw)**
- **6 small potatoes, halved and unpeeled**
- **1 large sweet potato, thickly sliced**
- **2 Small tomatoes cut in large chunks**
- **4-6 small, white baby-eggplant slit in quarters**
- **2 fresh whole garlic pods**
- **2 onions, finely chopped and crisply fried**

- **1 tsp salt**
- **½ tsp turmeric**
- **1 tsp red chili powder**
- **1 tsp coriander powder**
- **1 ½tsp cumin powder,**
- **1 tsp fresh ginger paste**
- **1 tsp fresh garlic paste**
- **2 tbsp tomato paste**
- **1 tbsp Kashmiri masala paste***
- **4 tbsp sunflower oil**

To prepare all the vegetables, wash and pat dry. Cut the onions, potatoes, sweet potatoes, and tomatoes into equal sized pieces. Slit the eggplants in quarters but do not cut through, keeping them intact.

In a large skillet or flat pan (with a lid, and around 35 cm/14 inch in diameter), layer the Paapri beans, cover with raw onion, potatoes, sweet potatoes, eggplants, tomatoes and whole garlic pods. Sprinkle the fried onion evenly all over.

Now evenly sprinkle all the dry ingredients; salt, turmeric, red chilli, coriander and cumin powders.

Add the ginger, garlic, tomato and Kashmiri masala pastes*.

Finally, dribble the oil all over.

Cover the lid and let it steam cook for 45 minutes. To test, poke the potato to check if soft and done.

Serve with warm rotli or crisp bread.

- The paaprie must be young and crisp. The strings on the sides must be peeled off. Larger ones tend to be tougher with thicker strings that are not easily chewable.
- Add small meatballs or fresh cleaned prawns toward the later part of the cooking
- Do not mix this dish with a spoon – only shake the pan to allow it to settle. Serve it in the same pan you cook it in for best visual appearance.
- Traditionally, 2 tsp carom seeds, locally referred to as Ajowan, were added to help digestion and prevent gas.

Kashmiri masala is a paste made up of many spices. It has a blend of red dried Kashmiri chillies, garlic, cumin, cinnamon, cardamom, nutmeg, oil and a few more ingredients and is readily available on most supermarket shelves in glass jars.

Main Dish
Teeji Vani

Rice Dishes – Chawal nu Bhonu

32. Marghi na Curry Chawal (Chicken Curry with Vegetable Palau)

36. Machi no Palau (Fish Biryani)

39. Machi no Sās Khichri (Lentil-rice and Fish in Tomato Gravy)

44. Jhinga na Curry Chawal (Shrimp coconut curry and rice)

47. Dhun Daar Pātiyo (Lentils with Rice and Prawn Chutney)

50. Jhinga no Palau (Prawn Biryani)

53. Dhansak (Brown Lentils and Meat with Brown Rice)

Rotli/ Dishes – Rotli nu Bhonu

59. Roast Gos (Sunday Lamb Roast)

62. Papeta ma gos for Ghambars (Potato and Meat Stew)

65. Sali Marghi (Chicken and Potato Straws)

68. Chicken Badami (Chicken Almond and Yogurt Curry)

Marghi na Curry Chawal
Chicken Curry with Vegetable Palau.

Marghi na Curry Chawal – Chicken Curry with Vegetable Palau

This particular dish is the simplest of curries. Easy to put together, this is the perfect introduction to curry making for a novice. It is my aunt Villie who introduced me to this delicious recipe.

Using a food processor to grind all the ingredients together and cooked in one pot, it leans on the traditional flavours using a rather unconventional method of preparing a typical curry. The results are simply divine!

6 to 8 servings

- **2 medium onions**
- **3 green chillies**
- **4 cm/1 ½ inch piece fresh ginger**
- **8 cloves of garlic, peeled**
- **3 tbsp oil**
- **1 ½ kg/ 3 ¼ lb chicken, bone-in, skinless cut in 8 pcs**
- **1 tsp salt**
- **1 tsp cumin powder**

- **2 tsp coriander powder**
- **¼ tsp turmeric**
- **1 tsp red chilli powder**
- **1-cup fresh tomato puree**
- **2 cups coconut milk**
- **3 tbsp fresh lemon juice**

- **Optional Ingredient:**
  2 tsp peanut butter

Grind together, in a food processor the onions, green chillies, fresh ginger and garlic.

In a large pot, heat the oil and add the ground mixture – fry until golden brown. To this, add the chicken and cook until it has browned; this will take 10-15 minutes. Now add all the dry ingredients of salt, cumin, coriander, turmeric and red chilli powders and mix well. Add to it the peanut butter (if using), tomato puree and coconut milk.

Mix well and bring to a boil for a few minutes. Cover the pan and lower heat. Cook for 30 minutes until the chicken has cooked through, and the curry is to a thick consistency or as desired. Add the lemon juice and cook another 5 minutes.

Tips

- This is served with a Vegetable Palau, which is full of amazing flavours. But it can be served with boiled Basmati rice or even Jasmine rice.
- Choose an onion, tomato, green chilli, coriander and cucumber salsa (Kachuber) for the basmati rice, and a mango salad on the side if served with the Jasmine rice
- The peanut butter can be omitted for those with nut allergy. It makes the curry thicker and creamier. For similar results, add sunflower seed or pumpkin seed butter.

Vegetable Palau

Vegetable Palau

This vegetable Palau is a perfect accompaniment to the Chicken Curry. And yet, it has so many wonderful flavours of its own making it a 'dish' often served by itself with just a simple raita or the dhansak ni dar (without meat).

6 to 8 servings

- 3 tbsp oil
- 2 medium onions finely chopped
- 1 tsp crushed garlic
- 2 tsp salt
- ¾ tsp ground cumin
- ¾ tsp ground cardamom
- ½ tsp ground cinnamon
- ¼ tsp ground cloves
- ¼ tsp turmeric powder
- 2 cups hard assorted vegetables like carrots, zucchini, green- beans etc., cleaned and diced

- 2 green chillies slit
- 2 cups basmati rice, thoroughly washed and starch removed
- 4 cups of water

- Mix together and keep aside at room temperature:

  1-cup thick yogurt

  1 tsp sugar

  ½ tsp salt

  ¼ tsp pinch of saffron

In a pot (preferably oven proof), heat the oil and fry the onions until golden brown. Add the garlic, salt and all the dry ground spices; cumin, cardamom, cinnamon, cloves, and turmeric powders. Sautee and stir this for a minute. Then add in the chopped vegetables and sauté for 3 minutes.

Now add in the rice and water. Cook until the rice is flaky and bubble holes form on top – approximately 20 minutes depending on the rice.

Layer the yogurt mixture on top of the rice and cover with foil and bake in a preheated 180 C/350 F degrees for 20 minutes. Optionally, cover tightly and cook on the stovetop, on a low flame for 20 minutes.

Tips

- Pick any 3 favourite vegetables. Green peas and yams are some of the other choices. It should look colourful and not get mushy.
- Yogurt should be at room temperature so it does not curdle on contact with the hot rice.
- The idea of putting it into the oven is to make it look presentable. Turn over the rice in your serving dish and then top it with the yogurt. Bake when you are ready to serve. It will save you time and trouble.

Machi no Palau
Fish Biryani

Machi no Palau – *Fish Biryani*

Unique to our family, the Machi no Palau (Fish Biryani) is an all-time favourite. In fact, my mother-in-law is well known amongst the community for her amazing recipe, which I share with her blessing.

When I was getting married, as a gesture of their affection toward me joining the family, my cousin-in-laws put me to the test: whether I was able to recreate this wonderful, aromatic, soul-satisfying dish. It is now a personal favourite in our home.

Since most of our friends and acquaintances have neither heard of this, nor tried it, we love to share this lovely dish at lunches, dinner parties, and special occasions.

6 to 8 servings

- **1 tbsp oil**
- **3 onions, finely chopped**
- **2 tsp garlic paste**
- **1 ½ tsp salt**
- **1 tsp cumin powder**
- **6 green chillies, finely chopped**
- **10 curry leaves**
- **2 medium tomatoes, finely chopped**
- **1 tsp chilli powder**
- **1 tsp curry powder**
- **½ tsp turmeric powder**
- **1-cup yogurt, with a pinch of sugar and salt at room temperature**

- **1 tsp garam masala**
- **Juice of 1 lemon or lime**
- **½ cup fresh coriander leaves, finely chopped**
- **½ tsp saffron threads, crushed**
- **¼ cup water**
- **3/4 kg/1 lb deboned, fish pieces**
- **3 cups basmati rice, thoroughly washed**
- **1 dry bay leaf**
- **2 thin sticks of cinnamon**
- **6 whole green cardamom pods, cracked open**
- **8 cups boiling hot water, well salted with 4 tsp salt**

For the Fish layer:

In a pan, heat the oil and fry the onions, until golden brown.

Add to this and stir a minute; garlic paste, salt, cumin powder, green chilies and curry leaves.

Now add to this and fry for 5-7 minutes; the tomatoes, chili, curry and turmeric powders.

Beat together and add to the pan:

1-cup yogurt at room temperature mixed with a pinch of sugar and a pinch of salt.

Let the mixture simmer over a medium-low heat for 20-30 minutes, until the spices are well cooked, and almost dry.
Initially cover the pan and after the time is done open the lid and dry off the masala stirring constantly over a higher heat.

Now add and bring to a boil the garam masala, lemon or lime, juiced, chopped fresh coriander leaves, saffron and the water. Add the fish, cut in squares and cook for 7 minutes or until fish is just cooked. Leave the pot uncovered at this time to ensure the gravy remains thick while the fish cooks through. If necessary, simply shake the pot and do not give it a stir at this stage.

For the rice:

In a large pan of boiling water (at least 8 cups), add the washed rice, bay leaf, cinnamon sticks and cardamom pods. Boil for 12 minutes or until rice is just cooked but not over-done. Remove and strain.

To assemble the Fish Palau:

In an ovenproof serving dish or pan, place half of the fish gravy and top with rice. Repeat with the rest of the fish gravy and rice.

With the back of a spoon make holes all over the top layer and drizzle a little saffron water. This will help bring a little colour to the pure white rice.

Cover and seal the pan well, ensuring no air escapes. Place the whole pot of Fish Biryani on a very low direct heat on the stovetop to simmer, or optionally place it in a preheated oven of 350 F/180 C degrees for 20 minutes. This ensures the flavour will steam through and the rice cooks evenly.

Tips

- It is best to use a firm fish like Salmon or Surmai. Haddock and Halibut are other alternates. Cutting them in thick squares keeps the fish from breaking apart.
- It is important to temper the yogurt with the cooked masala mixture while adding it in; add a few tablespoons of the hot masala mix into the yogurt before adding it all in. Alternately to play it safe, allow the mixture to cool down slightly before adding the yogurt to avoid any chance of curdling.
- Use full fat yogurt and not skimmed.
- For a colourful rice; make holes with the back of a spoon all over top layer and drizzle a little saffron mixed with a few drops of warm water. This will help bring a little colour to the pure white rice.
- Serve this with a Raita or Masala Dal if you wish. In my opinion it is perfect on its own.
- Weight measure of the rice is approximately 700 gm or 1 ½ lb.

Machi no Sas
Fish in Gravy

Machi no Sas – Fish in Gravy

Sās Khichri is a favourite in most Parsi homes. Made in a variety of ways, this version is a tomato-based spicy, sweet and sour dish. This is a prime example of the perfect Parsi Cooking Trinity of Tikhu, Khatu, Mithu (spicy, sour and sweet). Taste it before serving to perfect the fine balance that your family will enjoy! It is almost always served with Khichri rice.

In Mumbai, Machi nu Sās is often served as a side dish at wedding feasts without the khichri, as the Khichri itself is not served on happy occasions and hence omitted from this equation. However, the lagan no sās (wedding sauce) is different to this one, white in colour and not tomato based. It is prepared with small whole Pomfret fish and can easily be the best dish of the wedding feast!

This particular recipe is more or less Karachi-style, simple and easy to make and enjoyed by all.

Other versions add coconut milk and crushed onions.

6 to 8 servings

- 2 tbsp oil
- 2 tsp ginger paste
- 2 tsp garlic paste
- 2 tsp red chili powder
- 2 tsp cumin powder
- 4 tbsp plain flour
- 1 tsp salt
- 4 green chillies, slit

- 2 cups fresh tomato, pureed, preferably peeled and deseeded
- 3 cups water
- 2 eggs,
- 3 tbsp sugar
- 3 tbsp vinegar
- 1 kg /2.2 lb fillet of Salmon or any firm fish, cubed and lightly salted
- A handful of fresh coriander leaves, finely chopped

In a pan heat the oil and add the ginger and garlic paste, the chilli and cumin powders and the flour and salt. Mix the ingredients to make a roux; cook thoroughly.

Add and mix well, until smooth the fresh tomato puree and the water; bring the gravy to a boil and cook on a low fire, until thick. Add the slit green chillies.

Once thick, cool the gravy.

In bowl, beat well the eggs sugar and vinegar.

Add the egg mixture to the gravy, stirring it constantly on a low heat, and bring it to a boil.

Now add the fish and the finely chopped fresh coriander. Cover and cook for 5-7 minutes.

Serve with Khichri and a simple salad of radish and cucumber. Poppadoms are also generally an accompaniment to this dish, as is the Gajar mewa nu achar (carrot and dry fruit pickle).

- The only hurdle in this very simple recipe is when and how to add the egg. It can curdle and ruin the texture of this smooth sauce. For this it is best to wait for the sauce to cool down until tepid.

- If you are in a hurry make sure to "temper" the egg. To temper, put a spoonful of the sauce one at a time into the bowl of your beaten egg. Once the egg looks like it is properly incorporated with the sauce, slowly pour it all in to the main Sās. Keep mixing it all the time until you know it is cooked through.

- Keep aside the fish at room temperature, lightly salted, until ready to use.

- Substitute the plain flour with potato or gram flour to make this gluten free.

- Use an apple cider vinegar or fruit vinegar.

- Substitute the fish for fresh prawns or shrimp.

41

Khichri Rice
Rice and Lentil

Photo Courtesy Nafeesa Jalal

Khichri — Rice and Lentil

Khichri/Khichdi/Khichuri is derived from a Sanskrit word, simply meaning rice and lentil. It has many variations and is popularly referred to as a comfort food. Generally, its texture is wet rather than dry, similar to a risotto. It is often seasoned with clarified butter or pure ghee. From the Greeks to the Persians, it was a favourite of the Mughal Emperor Akbar!

Egyptians and their neighbours add vegetables to it, while the Indian sub-continent likes to serve it with yogurt or other forms of curries. Like the Parsis, other communities living on the shores of the Arabian Sea, Maharashtrians and the Sindhis tend to add shrimp to their Khichri, as do the Sri Lankans and Bangladeshis that thrive on the Bay of Bengal.

Healthy and simple, it is generally the first forms of solid food introduced to babies. Being affordable and a self-contained complete meal, it is also a food of the masses. Many cultures, including the Parsis, dedicate a meal of Khichri during their week of wedding festivities; yet it is deemed inauspicious to be served as part of the wedding feast or on the day off!

6 to 8 servings

- **1 tsp oil**
- **1 cinnamon stick**
- **3 green cardamom pods**
- **6 black cloves**
- **2 cups basmati rice, thoroughly washed**
- **½ cup red lentils, thoroughly washed**
- **1½ tsp salt**
- **⅓ tsp turmeric**
- **3 ½ cups of water**

In a pan, heat the oil. Add in and sauté for a few seconds, the cinnamon stick, cardamom and cloves.

Add to this the basmati rice, red lentils, salt, turmeric and water.

Cook on a high flame, until all the water is gone and you can see the rice through the bubbles. Lower the heat, cover tightly and steam for 20 minutes on a low flame. Serve hot.

Tips

- Adding ¼ cup of fried onions is an optional addition to this Khichri if desired.
- Red Lentils are split red masoor dal, orange in colour.

Thinga na Curry Chawal
Shrimp Coconut Curry with Rice

Jhinga na Curry Chawal – Shrimp Coconut Curry with Rice

Without a doubt, Parsis embrace Curry Chawal (literally, Curry Rice) as their own. A favourite in most Parsi homes, curry – especially the fish or prawn one – comes very close to Dhansak, and is also quintessentially Parsi.

"Curry" is a loose term used universally to describe a spicy sauce with meat, chicken, seafood or vegetables. It can be dry or wet; red, green, yellow or white in colour, depending on the spices added; coconut, yogurt or cream based and sometimes stock or broth is also added.

Tamil for 'sauce', the word "Kari" was anglicised in the 1700's by the British who colonised India. However, some records show the word "cury" which means cooking, to be a part of the Olde English language as early as 1300's.

Curry and rice is typically served with Kachumbar, a simple salad/salsa of onions, tomatoes, cucumbers and definitely a wedge of lemon.

Traditionally, this Shrimp or Prawn Curry is made shell-on, giving the curry its true authentic taste. If you know your guests are squeamish, shell the prawns, and add them on their own while cooking the curry. Remove them prior to adding the prawns and serving. Those eating the final dish will truly appreciate the time and trouble taken over this step. Alternatively, cook the curry with tail-on prawns or shrimp, keeping the taste with some compromise!

6 to 8 servings

- **1-cup desiccated or freshly scraped coconut**
- **6 large flat dry red chilies**
- **1 whole pod of fresh peeled garlic**
- **1/2 tsp sugar**
- **1 tsp salt**
- **2 tbsp coriander powder**
- **1 tbsp cumin powder**
- **¼ cup vinegar**

- **1 tsp oil**
- **1/2 tsp turmeric**
- **12 curry leaves**
- **2 green chillies, slit**
- **1-cup coconut water**
- **½ cup fresh tomato puree**
- **1 tsp tamarind paste or kokum paste**
- **1 kg/2.2 lb fresh prawns, shelled and deveined**

To make the curry paste, grind together until fine, the coconut and red chillies. Now add peeled garlic cloves, sugar, salt and the coriander and cumin powders with the vinegar to make into a paste.

In a pan, heat a tsp of oil and add turmeric, curry leaves and the green chillies. Gently stir for a minute and add the curry paste.

Now add the coconut water. Mix well and bring to a boil, and cover. Lower the heat and cook for 20 minutes.

Then add the fresh pureed tomatoes and the tamarind or kokum. Cover again and cook for another 30 minutes on a very low steam. If you are adding the shells of the prawns, add them now. At the end of this cooking time remove and discard the shells. Add the prawns and bring to a boil for 5 minutes, leaving the pot uncovered. Cover and close the stove. Let it rest for 10 minutes and serve with freshly boiled white rice.

- Substitute 1-cup of water for coconut water if unavailable.
- Add 1/2 cup of coconut milk to make it creamier if desired.
- Kokum are a small berry like a plant of the mangosteen family and is available dried in packets in most Indian stores. It is sour in taste.
- Tamarind grows in pods and these are dried, stoned and sold as a paste in blocks or bottles, commonly available in many supermarkets worldwide. It is sour in taste and often used in Thai, African and Indian cooking.
- If you cannot get tamarind paste or kokum, use the juice of one fresh lemon or lime.
- 2 tsp of chilli powder equals 6 large flat dry chillies, however grinding the red chillies adds to the colour and flavour.
- If adding the shells the weight of the prawns needed will be 1 ½ kg/3 lb.

Note: Curry Powder is not to be mistakenly affiliated to any Curry. Interestingly, Curry Powder was specifically mixed and boxed just for the Colonisers who were returning, allowing them to prepare their version of curry once back home. Many people use it in Mulligatawny soup for flavouring, and it is also used in Coronation Chicken.

Dhun Dar nay Patiyo
Golden Lentils and Rice with
Prawn Patia

Dhun Dar nay Patiyo — Golden Lentils and Rice with Prawn Patia

The basic meal of a typical Parsi household on any festive occasion is a trio of plain boiled rice, creamy golden lentils and thick chutney-like gravy called Patio; pronounced Pa-tea-O and not a patio.

It was combined to make it simple, quick and yet special. Healthy, ageless and timeless it continues to be the staple option of a menu on any occasion; birthdays, Navroze and even at religious ceremonies like the Navjote, Jashan and a wedding.

The Parsi Patio/Patia is a choice of fish or prawn/shrimp and not of any poultry or meats. However, a version is made up of eggplants; which is also just as delicious. To get it just right, one has to perfectly balance the Parsi Cooking Trinity of tikhu-khatu-mithu (spice-sour-sweet).

6 to 8 servings

For the dar (lentils):

- 1-cup/250 gm tuar dal/pigeon peas (not oily), thoroughly washed
- 1-cup/250 gm red split masoor dal, thoroughly washed
- ¾ tsp turmeric
- 1 tsp salt
- 125 gm/4 oz salted butter

Wash the lentils and place in a stockpot with 4 cups of water. Add the turmeric and salt to it. Bring to a boil and cook on a medium heat for 40 minutes or until cooked through. The water can be topped up if necessary.

Add the butter and pulse the lentils to a thick, liquid mash and until smooth.

For the Jhinga no Patiyo:

- 1 tbsp oil
- 1 tsp ginger paste
- 2 tsp garlic paste
- 1 ½ tsp salt
- 2 tsp red chilli powder
- ¾ tsp turmeric powder
- 4 medium to large tomatoes, crushed
- 1 kg/2.2 lb onions, thinly sliced, fried golden brown
- ½ tsp garam masala
- 2 raw mangoes, peeled
- 1 tbsp jaggery
- 1 kg/2.2 lb raw peeled prawns, washed and lightly salted

In a large pan, heat a tbsp of oil and stir in the ginger, garlic, salt, red chilli and turmeric powders. Add the tomatoes, fried onions and a stir. Then add the garam masala and raw mangoes.

Cover and cook on a low fire until the "oil separates" and shows like little droplets on the sides of the pan. This will take about 30 minutes.

Now add the crushed jaggery; let it melt and mix well. Add the shelled prawns and allow it to simmer for 7 minutes. Keeping the cover tightly sealed, let it rest for 10 minutes before serving.

Tips

- The pātiyo is not meant to be liquid nor dry. It will be done and ready when you see the drops of oil on the side of the pan. This is called "tayl per avay".
- Once you add the jaggery for sweetness the entire pātiyo will have a beautiful shiny glaze over it. Now you are ready to add the prawns and finish off the dish.
- For the perfect end result, taste for thiku-khatu-mithu /spicy, sour and sweet!
- Have the leftovers, if any, with a warm rotli and freshly sliced onion on the side. It is yummy!

Did you know?

The pātiyo is also used in reference to a particular kind of pot used as a cooking utensil. It is the actual shape of the vessel that denotes the name. Wide and flat but with bulging rounded sides is the best way I can describe it.

Serve in 3 separate dishes of Boiled Basmati Rice, Lentils and the Patio.

Jhinga no palao
Prawn Biryani

Photo Courtesy Nafeesa Jalal

Jhinga no Palau – Prawn Biryani

Parsis tend to call this dish Jhinga no Palau, but it is really a Prawn Biryani. The subtle difference between the two is very simple: Palau is generally rice boiled in a broth/stock. It is rather delicately flavoured and has very few spices. Biryani, on the other hand, has many more ingredients. The rice is par boiled in fresh salted water; a bay leaf and a few pods of cardamom are also tossed in to season the rice. Once the water is strained out, saffron (or yellow colouring) is added for a yellow hue to some of the rice.

Biryani is often served at wedding feasts and auspicious occasions like birthdays and anniversaries. It has stronger spicier flavours and generally served with a yogurt raita to cool the palate. Some people like to serve it with a spicy masala dal (spicy lentils) similar to the "dhansak" (although meatless), to add to the spiciness!

6 to 8 servings

- **1-cup of fried onion**
- **2 large tomatoes**
- **6 green chillies**
- **Half a bunch of fresh coriander leaves, about 1 cup**
- **1 generous tsp salt**
- **Saffron threads**
- **1 flat tsp cumin powder**
- **Pinch of turmeric**
- **2 flat tsp red chilli powder**
- **½ tsp coriander powder**
- **2 small green mango, peeled and chopped**

- **Pinch of sugar**
- **½ tsp garam masala**
- **1 tbsp oil**
- **1 kg/2.2 lb peeled, raw prawns; washed and lightly salted**
- **½ cup yogurt with a pinch of salt and sugar**
- **8 cups boiling water, salted with 3 tsp salt**
- **2 ½ cups rice**
- **3 tsp salt**
- **2 whole cardamom pods**
- **1 bay leaf**

For The Prawn Masala

In a food processor pulse together: the fried onions, tomatoes, green chillies, coriander leaves, salt, saffron, cumin, turmeric, red chilli powder, coriander powder, green mango, sugar and garam masala.

In a pot, heat a little oil and fry the mixture; lower heat and cover, simmering for 25 minutes until the oil separates. You will see the tiny beads of oil on the side of the pan above the 'masala'.

Add to this 1 kg/2.2 lb peeled, raw prawns (washed and lightly salted). Cover and cook for 10 minutes or until just cooked.

Remove from heat and cool the mixture; until just warm.

Add ½ cup yogurt mixed with a pinch of salt and sugar. Mix well.

For the Rice

Boil in water (at least 8 cups) until just cooked; rice, salt, cardamom pods and a bay leaf.

Strain the rice.

In a large pot, place alternative layers of the prawns cooked in the spices and rice. Sprinkle a small pinch of saffron; this will give a beautiful hue of yellow colours. Cover tightly and steam for 30 minutes. Serve on a platter.

Tips

- If green mangoes are unavailable, substitute the sourness with the juice of a lemon or lime. Add this after the prawns are cooked. Sometimes the prawns turn hard with lemon juice if applied while they are raw.
- Add a few drops of oil if you like your Biryani to have each grain of rice singularly visible, referred to in Parsi cooking as "khulo dano". You can add this before or after draining the rice. You can also prefer to rinse the cooked rice in cold water immediately after straining them. This ensures the gluten is washed away and stops it from sticking together.
- There is enough flavour and moisture to serve this dish on its own. Alternately serve a raita or masala dal (spicy lentils) with it on the side.
- I often prepare double the masala and freeze half of it for later use.

Dhansak

Dhansak – *Meat cooked in lentils with rice*

Food being the number one priority for most Parsis, the infamous Dhansak is a favourite dish and it is best described as a speciality. Being both tedious and time-consuming to prepare, as well as heavy to digest, Dhansak is generally left for a treat and more traditionally, for a Sunday afternoon lunch. Families gather for the meal and get-together, followed by a siesta!

There are many versions and stories of its origins, both in name and in ingredients. But like most recipes, it has evolved over time and geography. I believe that it originates from our Persian roots, mimicking the Khoresh, a stew that was made up of lentils, spinach, plums and meat, served on a bed of rice with an array of mokhalafat or sides. Once we migrated to India, it turned to Dhansak; Dhan meaning golden/gold or wealth and Sak/sag/shak meaning greens or vegetables.

We continue to use golden lentils and add lots of vegetables, greens and others to make the dish today. The plums used to make it sweet and sour are now tamarind and jaggery. Another common addition is the locally abundant raw mango. The spinach has changed to coriander leaves and we have added a wealth of fragrant spices that have been blended into various "Dhansak masala mixes" in order to cut down on the long list of ingredients.

Lamb and mutton are what gives the Dhansak its true flavours. We often see that chicken has been substituted for meat, especially in the West. But I personally would not recommend that.

Continuing the practice of the ancient Persian tradition of serving this dish with many sides, Dhansak is served with caramelised brown rice which is dressed with small prawn or meat kebabs, freshly sliced onions in a date and tamarind sauce, a kuchumbar made up of finely diced tomato, onion, cucumber and green chilli, tossed with salt and vinegar. In addition, some households have cooked beet slices, lemon wedges, ambakaliyo (sweet chutney made with green mango) or murumbo (sweet chutney made with bottle gourd) are also offered.

There is no right or wrong to cooking Dhansak, and each family has its own ingredients and methods for this historic dish. Love of Dhansak just seems to endorse one's "Parsi-pannu" or Parsi-ness. Serve this with a chilled beer or shandy for the ultimate Parsi eating experience!

6 to 8 servings

Step 1 – Lentils

In a large pot boil together for 1.5 hours:

- **13 oz/375 gm Toor/tuar lentils, washed**
- **4 oz/125 gm of red masoor lentils, washed**
- **¾ tsp turmeric**

- **1 tsp salt**
- **8 cups water**
- **125 gm/4 oz of salted butter**

Add the butter to the pot half way through the cooking.

Once cooked, cool the lentil mix. Using an immersion blender, a food processor, liquidiser or a large sieve, form a smooth pulp. Leave aside.

Note:

If the lentils are soaked for an hour or two, they will cook very quickly.

Step 2 – Broth

In a second pot, boil together until the meat is tender, making sure there is at least 1-cup of stock left over:

- **1 kg/2.2 lb lamb or mutton or goat, bone-in, cut into big pieces**
- **1 tsp salt**
- **10 cups of water**

Step 3 – Masala

In a wet grinder, blend until smooth:

- **2 tsp garlic paste**
- **1 tsp ginger paste**
- **8 large dry red Kashmiri chillies or 2½ tsp chilli powder**
- **4 green chillies**
- **1 tsp cumin powder**
- **1 tsp dhansak masala**
- **2 tsp jaggery**

- **1-cup finely chopped fried onions**
- **3 tomatoes, finely chopped**
- **1 tsp tamarind paste**
- **1-cup fresh coriander leaves**
- **6 fresh mint leaves**
- **1 tbsp oil**

Now in a third pot, fry the masala mixture on a low flame, stirring constantly. When done, you will see tiny droplets of oil released from the sides of the pan at the edges. Do not keep the flame on high. Keep stirring it. Remove this from the stovetop after 3 minutes.

Step 4 – Assembly

- **Fried masala**
- **Cooked lentils**
- **1-cup meat stock**
- **Cooked pieces of meat**
- **2 raw green mangoes peeled and cut, if available**

Add the fried masala above to the pot of lentils, and bring it to a boil. Add a few pieces of peeled green mangoes for sourness, if available.

Then add 1-cup of the stock from the pot of meat, and bring to a boil. Cook until the lentils are of the consistency you desire.

Now add the meat, cover the pan and let it simmer for 30 minutes. Do not let it boil since the dal will now start to stick at the bottom of the pan. It is a necessary step to infuse the flavours of the meat.

Serve with brown rice, freshly sliced onions or kachumber, fresh lemon wedges, beetroots, murumba and last but not least, a chilled beer or shandy to accompany this meal.

Tips

- The chillies in this recipe are for an average milder dhansak. Add chillies and chilli powder according to your taste.
- Dhansak is supposed to be a bit spicy.
- Toor or Tuar is also called split pigeon peas. They are golden in colour. They are oily or plain. I use the plain variety as it is easier to digest.
- If the lentils are soaked for an hour or two, they will cook very quickly.
- Fatty meat was used for this dish, but since we only use lean meats, butter has been added. You may halve the butter if your meat has fat on it.
- Dhansak, like many other Parsi and Persian dishes tastes better the next day, giving it time to 'mature' overnight.
- All Dhansak recipes differ and many have vegetables like eggplant, aubergine, potato, raw onions, butternut squash and pumpkin. I have only ever used pumpkin in mine over the years. If you wish, add one cup of finely chopped pumpkin in the lentils while cooking it. Most do not add jaggery but I enjoy it as it brings the dish together perfectly.

Brown Rice

Brown Rice

Not to be confused with brown rice that is whole grain rice with husks on, this brown rice gets its colour from caramelised onions, giving a slight sweetness that helps balance the spice of the Dhansak.

- **2 tsp brown sugar**
- **1 tbsp oil**
- **1 long cinnamon stick**
- **8 cloves**
- **8 black peppercorns**

- **3 whole green cardamom pods**
- **3 flat tsp salt**
- **3 cups basmati rice, thoroughly washed to remove starch**
- **6 cups of water**

In a pan, heat and caramelise the sugar. The colour should be fairly dark. Immediately add the oil, the whole spices and salt.

Add all the washed rice and the water. Bring to a boil on a high flame. Keep a watchful eye, when the rice starts showing through the water, lower the heat, cover and steam the rice for 22-25 minutes. With a fork gently fluff up the cooked rice right away, to keep it separated. Serve.

Tips

- Keep all the ingredients ready before you start.
- Always use cold water.
- Add a bay leaf if you like.
- Try the perfect-rice-finger-test! Put your index finger on the very top of the rice. Gently pour water until the first indentation cut of your finger. This always seems to work!
- The colour of the rice will depend on how dark your caramel is.
- Do not soak the rice, as it will over-cook.

Masala Roast Gos served with Potatoes and Eggs

Roast Gos – Sunday Lamb Roast

The traditional Sunday Roast dates back to the 15th century, at the table of Henry VII where roasted pieces of beef were served to the King and his guards (Yeoman Warders, nicknamed the 'Beefeaters'), after church. But Sunday Roast wasn't just for royalty – common folk would drop off their beef on the way to church to be roasted in local bakery ovens, and collected on their way back home. Today, variations of Sunday Roasts are eaten in the UK, and all over the world.

Whereas the roast meat was traditionally beef, the Australians carried on this tradition with lamb, and today, many of us are spoilt for choice and can cater to everyone's palate – roast chicken, pork, and even a 'nut' roast (for the vegetarians). A traditional roast is served with roast potatoes (brought over by the Spanish from Peru in the 15th Century), Yorkshire pudding, and other vegetables such as carrots, parsnips, and cabbage, and served with lots of gravy. Condiments such as horseradish for beef, mint jelly for lamb, cranberry jelly and mustard for pork or chicken often find their way to the table.

But even the most splendid traditional roast can use a twist once in a while: bringing together sub-continental flavours and British traditions, this Parsi-style roast lamb will be sure to please everyone. Succulent and bursting with flavour, this roast is really for any day of the week, for a dinner party, or to share with your family. Easy to prepare ahead of time, the roast can be marinated and frozen. The juices form into a light gravy. Serve with roasted potatoes and hardboiled eggs for a real Parsi experience.

6 to 8 servings

- **1-cup of yogurt**
- **4 garlic cloves, freshly grated**
- **1 tbsp freshly ground ginger**
- **1 tbsp freshly grated lime zest**
- **1/4 cup fresh lime juice**
- **2 tsp salt**
- **1 ½ tsp red chilli powder**

- **1 ½ tsp coriander powder**
- **1 tsp cumin powder**
- **½ tsp turmeric**
- **1 tsp garam masala**
- **½ tsp mustard powder**
- **3 kg/6.6 lb leg of lamb, washed and patted dry**

For The Marinade

In a bowl mix together the yogurt, garlic, ginger, lime zest, fresh lime juice, salt, red chilli, coriander, cumin, turmeric, garam masala and mustard powders.

Rub the marinade all over the leg of lamb. Let it marinate overnight. Bring it back to room temperature before you start cooking. Place the roast on a very large sheet of foil, placed in a large dish with sides.

Preheat the oven to 190 C/375 F degrees and cook uncovered for 30 minutes. Turn the roast over. Bring the temperature down to 175 C/350 F degrees. Bring the sides of the foil up and cover the meat completely, trying to make a 'tent' of the foil to allow the steam to flow through. Cook for another 3 hours. Check if the lamb is really soft and coming off the bone. Let it stand covered for 10 minutes before serving.

- Keep a bit of the fat on the leg of lamb to keep it moist through the long hours of cooking.
- The hind leg of lamb is softer than the front legs.
- Massage the marinade into the meat with your hands, it will make a difference. (Wear a pair of gloves if you prefer).
- If you do not wish to cook the meat on the day of purchase you can freeze it for 30 days after marinating. Defrost the meat for 24 hours in the refrigerator before cooking. Do not refreeze already frozen meat.
- The yogurt must be thick and not at all watery.
- When cooking with yogurt at high heat the end result is always a curdled look. If you prefer smoother gravy to serve, it is best to remove the roast to a platter and tip all the gravy into a pan. Use an immersion blender, reheat the gravy and pour all over the roast or serve it on the side. Optionally, add a pinch of crushed saffron threads when reheating the gravy. It adds to the richness and aromas leaving the gravy with a beautiful colour as well.

Papayta ma Gos
(Ghambar nu Gos)

Papayta ma Gos (Ghambar nu Gos) – Meat with Potatoes

As I stepped into adult life and started cooking for my family, I soon realised food was really all about comfort.

Favourites were always easier to cook than others. Challenges were always my personal best. And so, I was introduced to my mother-in-law's wonderful cooking.

This recipe is most sought-after, and rather popular in our large extended family. It has been passed on from my husband's wonderful maternal grandmother and later through his mum to me. Everyone who cooks daily already knows, for those using a "hand" as a measuring spoon, it is hard to write or teach a recipe. But determined on mastering this classic, I managed to pursue and to learn the secrets of this great recipe.

While I would literally "catch" the spices from her hand into a measuring spoon to jot down the exact amount, it was both good fun and a feat in itself! I knew I had nailed it when she was kind enough to tell me I could make it better than her; just her gentleness oozing out as she still makes the BEST ever Papayta ma Gos. Thanks to my mother-in-law for always being genuinely proud of my every achievement and for always being my "go to" person. I am truly blessed to call her too.

6 to 8 servings

- 2 tbsp oil
- 1 kg/2.2 lb pieces of meat
- 2 tsp ginger paste
- 4 tsp garlic paste
- 1 ½ tsp salt
- 2 tsp red chilli powder
- 1/2 tsp cumin powder
- 4 slit green chillies
- Water, as required
- 2 cinnamon sticks

- 10 black peppercorns
- 10 cloves
- 6 green cardamoms
- 400 gm/1 lb finely sliced onions, fried until golden brown
- 400 gm/1 lb tomatoes, peeled and chopped
- 1 tbsp oil
- 750 gm/ 1½ lb peeled potatoes, cut small-pieces
- Salt to taste

Heat 2 tbsp oil in a large deep skillet add and brown, 1 kg/2.2lb pieces of meat (see tips); this will take 10 minutes.

Add to the meat, the ginger and garlic paste, salt, chilli and cumin powders and the green chillies. Keep mixing, adding a tablespoon of water if it starts to stick.

Add all the dry whole spices, cinnamon, black peppercorns, cloves and green cardamoms.

Mix well and add the fried onions and peeled tomatoes. Bring to a boil and lower the heat. Cover the pan and let it cook until meat is almost tender.

For The Potatoes

In a separate pan or baking sheet, fry or roast until golden the peeled potatoes with the oil. Lightly salt. Remove from any excess oil and add to the meat. Cover and simmer for 15-20 minutes.

Serve hot with rotli or crisp bread.

Tips

- Use lamb, goat or mutton with bone. This recipe generally calls for larger pieces. The bones give the dish its flavour. It must cook until very tender.
- If needed, add up to ½ cup water at some point. The end result should be thick gravy.
- If roasting the potatoes, toss them in 2 tbsp of oil before placing in the oven. Use the left over oil from the fried onions. Salt the potatoes lightly as soon as they come out of the oven for best results.
- Frying onions prior to the cooking always helps as it takes up a lot of time. Keep them flat in freezer bags frozen for up to 3 months.

Murghi ma Sali
Chicken with Potato Straws

Murghi Ma Sali – Chicken with Potato Straws

This dish is part of a Parsi Wedding Feast called "Patra nu bhonu," served on fresh large banana leaves. With large numbers of guests in attendance, service is done in numerous "seatings". Generally 100-150 people sit at one time in each of these "seatings", taking turns to ensure that every guest has been served. Food at weddings is still often served on banana leaves as it is not only traditional, but the leaves are readily available, and do not create excess waste as they are easily compostable.

This chicken dish has subtle spices and delicious gravy that can be enjoyed with warm rotli. Originally, the dish was made with whole dried apricots, instead of the potato straws and is referred to as Jardaloo ma murghi (Chicken with dried apricots). Personally, I prefer the recipe below but have included the variation with apricots too. Either way, this dish is a timeless Parsi classic.

6 to 8 servings

- 2 tbsp oil
- 8 pieces of skinless chicken
- 1 tsp fresh ginger paste
- 1 tsp fresh garlic paste
- 1 tsp red chilli powder
- ½ tsp turmeric powder
- 1 tsp cumin powder
- 1 tsp salt
- 2 whole cardamoms
- 1 stick cinnamon

- 2 green chillies slit open
- 6 black peppercorns
- 6 cloves
- 1-cup fried golden brown onions
- 2 tomatoes, quartered
- Water
- 500 gm/1 lb of ready-to-eat plain potato straws
- Optional Ingredients:
  12-18 pieces of dry baby apricots
  A handful of fresh coriander leaves

In a pan, heat the oil and lightly brown all the chicken, for approximately 7 minutes. Add the spices, the onions, the tomatoes and a few tablespoons of water and mix well.

Now add the dry apricots (if using), give it a stir, and cover the pot. Cook for 30 minutes until all the chicken pieces are cooked through. The gravy should be thick.

Add a handful of finely chopped coriander leaves (if using) and for about 5 minutes.

Sprinkle the 500 gm/1lb ready to eat potato straws all over just before serving.

Tips

- Cook uncovered if you want to dry the gravy on a high flame for a couple of extra minutes.
- Buy a packet of ready to eat thin crisp potato straws. Add these at the very end to keep the crunchy texture.

- The colour of the gravy will depend on the onion, the darker the onion has been fried the deeper the colour.
- You can add ¾ cup tomato purée instead of pieces if you like a thicker sauce. However, this dish authentically calls for clearer lighter gravy. The smoothness and coarseness depends on the onion and tomato.
- Purée accordingly and use a food processor if you prefer.

Chicken Badami
Almond and Yogurt Curry

Chicken Badami — Almond and Yogurt Curry

The combination of braised meat, yogurt and nuts make a good Korma/Qorma. Generally with lots of gravy and oil or ghee, it is a dish relished in the subcontinent. Persians and Turks have their own versions of the same. Originated in the 1600's the Mughal Dynasty made it popular and called it the Shahi Qorma, i.e. Royal Qorma by adding saffron, cream, and assorted nuts – very royal indeed!

Fortunately, Korma does not always have to be topped with oil or ghee to make it perfect. A Parsi version of this recipe omits the use of excess oil and instead uses ground almonds and yogurt for richness. Delicious in flavour, thick in texture with a beautiful caramel colour, this version of the original Persian Korma is a favourite in our home.

Simple ingredients and easy to make, enjoy this Chicken Badami with a warm naan.

6 to 8 servings

- 1 tbsp oil
- 1 dry bay leaf
- 1 tsp fresh ground garlic
- 1 tsp fresh ginger
- 1 tsp salt
- 1 1/2 tsp red chilli powder
- 1 tsp cumin powder
- 1 tsp coriander powder
- 1/4 tsp turmeric

- 10-12 pieces of chicken, skinless but with bone
- 1 large tomato
- 4 green chillies
- 1-cup water
- 1-cup thick yogurt with a pinch of salt and a pinch of sugar
- ½ cup ground almonds
- ½ tsp garam masala

In a pan, heat oil. Add to this, the bay leaf, fresh ground garlic and ginger paste, salt, red chilli, cumin, coriander and turmeric powders. Give it a stir and add the pieces of chicken, skinless but with bone.

Brown together for a few minutes on low heat, making sure the spices do not burn and the chicken changes colour.

In a processor, blend the tomato, green chillies and 1-cup water.

Add to the chicken and bring to a boil. Cover the pan and cook for 30 minutes until the chicken is cooked through. Open the lid, turn the stove on high and let all the water evaporate until only one cup of thick gravy remains. Bring the pan off the stove and let it cool until just warm.

Mix together in a bowl, yogurt with a pinch of salt and a pinch of sugar, ground almonds and the garam masala. Add the mixture of the yogurt into the cooled chicken.

The Korma is now ready. Reheat gently. Serve with naan.

- Chicken is best cooked when at room temperature and not cold or frozen.
- Keep the yogurt mixture at room temperature prior to use.
- The pieces of leg and thigh with bone will take the said amount of time in this recipe. Breast meat cooks quicker and boneless at a different time. Adjust accordingly.
- Substituting Chicken for bone-in Lamb/Mutton/Goat Meat will also make this just as delicious if preferred.
- Ground almonds are available in most Indian stores, health food stores, and supermarkets. This is made from peeled almonds. For nut allergies substitute freshly ground sunflower seeds. It is just as delicious!
- Use fresh tomatoes for the purée.
- When possible, grind your cumin and coriander seeds for freshness, and make your own fresh ginger and garlic paste. It is worth the results.
- This dish can be prepared 2 days ahead and refrigerated.

Desserts
Mithoo Monu

72. Parsi Custard (Traditional Wedding Custard)

74. Doodh Pak (Almond and Rice Pudding)

76. Mango Ice-cream

78. Kulfi (Burnt Milk Ice-cream)

80. Ravo (Semolina and Egg Pudding)

A serving of
Parsi Lagan nu Custard

Parsi Lagan nu Custard – Wedding Custard

Traditionally, Parsi weddings are large events where all the elders of the community are invited, and the weeklong pre-wedding ceremonies are celebrated with close family and friends. Different menus are set for each ceremony and the finale is of course the Patra nu Bhonu or Wedding Feast!

Served on long tables and eaten on banana leaves, the Wedding Feast is a menu of 7 to 11 courses. This square of custard pudding, served at the end of it all, is much looked forward to. Prepared in large trays, it is relatively simple to make and cut into simple squares to serve. Although simple, this dessert is not to be misunderstood, as it is rich in taste and texture and most worthy of a Wedding Dinner!

Makes 12 squares

- **6 cups of whole milk**
- **½ cup sugar**
- **Pinch of salt**
- **One tin of evaporated milk (11 oz/325 ml)**
- **One tin of condensed milk (7 oz/200 ml)**
- **One slice of plain soft white bread, broken into crumbs**
- **½ cup grated or finely chopped pistachios**
- **½ cup ground almonds (blanched)**
- **2 tsp vanilla essence**
- **2 tsp ground cardamom**
- **6 lightly beaten eggs, sieved**

In a large pot, heat the milk with the sugar, salt, and both, the evaporated and condensed milk.

Mix well until dissolved. Bring to a boil and cook for 15 minutes.

Now add bread crumbs, pistachios and almonds. Let the mixture boil for another 15 minutes. Then remove from the heat and cool through.

Add to the cooled mixture, the vanilla essence, cardamom powder and the lightly beaten eggs through a sieve. Mix well.

Heat the oven to 160 C/325 F. Pour the mixture into a 33x22cm/13x9" flat baking dish. Place the dish in a water bath and bake for 30 minutes or until just set.

Serve warm or cold.

Tips

- It is important to bake on a low heat so the eggs do not curdle at any point. It must wobble when you turn the oven off allowing for nice soft custard.
- Sieve the eggs to ensure the silky smooth pudding.

Doodh Pak
Milky Almond and Rice Pudding

74

Doodh Pak — Milky Almond and Rice Pudding

Every culture seems to have its own version of rice pudding, and Parsis are no exception! A simple and healthy dessert to serve at family meals or for larger crowds, Doodh Pak is a milky almond and rice pudding, flavoured with vanilla or rose water, and cardamom powder. It is often served with fresh puris (fried bread).

6 to 8 servings

- **8 cups whole milk**
- **1-cup plus 1 tbsp of sugar**
- **½ cup crushed almond powder, peeled**
- **½ cup crushed raw rice grains**
- **1 tsp salt**

- **1 tin of evaporated milk (11 oz/325 ml)**
- **1 ½ tsp crushed freshly ground cardamom**
- **4 tbsp rose water**
- **2 tsp vanilla**
- **¼ cup slivered almonds, to garnish**

In a large pot, heat the milk and stir in the sugar until it is all dissolved. Bring to a boil and then add the ground almond and crushed rice. Lower the heat and allow this to cook for half an hour, stirring from time to time.

Now add the salt and evaporated milk and cook for another 30 minutes, still on a low heat. The mixture should be thickened and creamy. Add the ground cardamom, rose water and vanilla.

To serve, garnish with roasted slivered almonds.

Tips

- The pudding will thicken a bit once it is cool. It tastes delicious cold or warm. It is a personal preference. Ideally, it is served chilled with hot, fresh and soft puris.

Mango Ice cream

Mango Ice Cream

Sounds rather simple, but when made with the best mangoes, this ice cream is absolutely divine. My fondest memories of eating this homemade mango ice cream include waiting for my uncle to finish cranking the ice cream churner, a large wooden tub, with a huge metal cylinder. All of us cousins would help with breaking the large cube of ice, constantly topping the tub with rock salt and ice pieces, producing an incredible dessert. It brings back a flood of very happy memories!

6 to 8 servings

- **1-cup milk**
- **4 egg yolks**
- **12 oz/355 ml condensed milk**

- **20 oz/590 ml whipping cream**
- **2 kg/4.4 lb sweet mango pulp, weighed after peeled and cut**
- **¼ tsp salt**

In a pan whisk together the milk and egg yolks. Scald, and keep stirring on a low flame until the mixture thickens and feels heavy while mixing. Do not let it boil.

Cool the mixture.

Add the condensed milk, the cream, mango and salt. Taste for sweetness. Chill in the fridge or freezer and churn in an ice cream machine. Alternatively, freeze mixture but keep mixing from time to time until it sets together. Serve scooped with fresh peeled diced mangoes.

Tips

- It is best to use a flavourful sweet mango to get a great taste. Anveratol and Alphonso are the best two choices. Langra has also got a good strong flavour.
- When fresh mangoes are not accessible there are a variety of mango pulp available canned.
- If you need to enhance a flat taste, add a little fresh lemon or lime juice, and an additional dash of salt. Try the mixture for a final taste when it is cold just before you are about to add it to the ice cream machine.
- The consistency and texture is best when eaten freshly churned. It has no ice particles nor is it hard, so simply melts in the mouth.

Kulfi
Burnt milk ice cream with nuts

Kulfi — Burnt milk ice cream with nuts

This burnt milk ice cream, often served as a cone-shaped ice-lolly, is creamy, rich and flavourful – perfect for cooling the palate after a spicy meal or on a hot summer's day. Made with full fat milk, and flavoured with nuts and cardamom, it is laborious but the end result is heavenly.

6 to 8 servings

- **12 cups full cream milk, room temperature**
- **½ cup finely ground pistachios**
- **¼ cup finely blanched ground almonds**
- **½ cup finely ground pistachios**
- **¼ tsp salt**
- **1½ cups of sugar**

- **½ cup full cream milk, cold**
- **4 tbsp corn flour or cornstarch**
- **2 tsp ground cardamoms**
- **1 tsp vanilla essence**
- **Optional ingredient:**
- 1 tsp crushed saffron

Boil the milk on a low fire until it reduces to about 8 cups.

Remove from heat and add in the almonds and pistachios, salt and the sugar. Stir well until the sugar has dissolved and place the pot back on the heat. Keep mixture boiling until it reduces another cup or so.

Remove from the heat and let it rest for 10 minutes.

In a small bowl mix the corn flour or starch with the cold milk until smooth. Add this to the mixture and stir well. Also add the cardamom and the vanilla, and saffron if using.

Return to heat and keep stirring constantly until the mixture thickens. Boil the mixture for a full minute to ensure the corn starch is cooked through. Remove from the heat.

Cool properly and chill for a few hours in the fridge. Now fill the kulfi cone-shaped containers and freeze.

Tips

- The mixture needs to be thickened just right so the nuts do not sink to the bottom of the cone.
- If cones are not accessible, use ice-lolly moulds, or a flat box in which you can cut squares, or even large ice cube trays.

Ravo on a Sagun ni thali

Ravo – Semolina and Egg Pudding

A semolina and egg pudding, Parsis tend to prepare Ravo for all auspicious occasions including Navroze (New Year), birthdays, jashans (prayers), weddings and anniversaries.

Ravo is also often a part of a toddler's daily diet, since it is nutritious and healthy. Referred to as "Sagun-nu" or something that is auspicious, most families have their own recipes passed down from generation to generation. This is from my mother's private collection of recipes and much admired. She has often been requested to prepare huge amounts for celebrations for many of her friends and family. All her grandchildren still consider Ravo made by her hand to be the best, even if the recipe is followed to a tee by others!

6 to 8 servings

- **125 gm/4 oz salted butter**
- **125 gm/4 oz coarse semolina**
- **140 gm/5 oz sugar**
- **3 eggs, room temperature**
- **2 cups milk, keep more to add**
- **1 tsp vanilla essence**

- **Pinch of salt**
- **1 flat tsp ground cardamom**
- **1 tbsp oil to fry**
- **¼ cup slivered almonds**
- **¼ cup raisins**
- **Optional ingredient:**
  1 tsp ground nutmeg

In a pot, melt the butter on a low heat. Add the semolina and fry until fragrant and pinkish in colour, stirring constantly for about 5 minutes. Add the sugar and mix well. Remove from heat and set aside.

In a bowl, beat the eggs and a little milk with a fork; strain it through a sieve and into the pan, mixing constantly so that it does not all curdle.

Return the pan to a low heat and add about 2 cups of milk. Keep mixing until the mixture thickens and coats the back of your spoon.

Now add vanilla essence, salt, ground cardamom, ground nutmeg, and mix.

In a pan heat the oil, add the slivered almonds until it just turns colour and add the raisins for a few seconds. Remove on a kitchen paper towel to drain the grease. To serve, sprinkle the Ravo with the fried raisins and almond slivers.

Tips

- The texture of the Ravo will depend on the semolina, the finer it is the less textured it will be. I prefer the coarsest semolina.
- Taste for vanilla essence.

- After frying the almonds and raisins, leave on a paper towel to drain before sprinkling. To fry, gently heat the oil, add the almonds and after a minute add the raisins for less than a minute. Keep a plate ready to overturn immediately. It will burn rather quickly!

- Add more milk to soften as and when needed. It will harden as it cools.

- Keep the eggs at room temperature and the milk tepid warm to help you along.

- Use a whisk to stir as it prevents the lumps.

Tea Time Snacks

Choi ni Satheh

84. Parsi Choi (Tea)

86. Batasa (Parsi Butter Biscuit)

89. Kumas (Parsi Cake)

92. Khatai (Parsi Sweet Biscuits)

95. Chaapat (Parsi Sweet Pancakes)

98. Malido

Parsi Choi

Photo Courtesy Sheeraz Wania

84

Parsi Choi – Parsi Tea

Tea is a very vital part of the daily routine for most. The strength and taste of the tea is indispensable for Parsis and for most people hailing from the sub-continent. Many Parsis like their tea flavoured with mint leaves and even lemongrass blades called lilly choi, making their cup of tea perfect.

Natives of the Indian sub-continent believe tea to be an integral part of their daily diet. Breakfast is generally a cup of sweet tea with bread for dunking. In India, Pakistan and Bangladesh and perhaps other neighbouring countries too, there are roadside Dhabas – teahouses that send their staff with already prepared tea to run through government offices on a daily basis. This is to provide the workers their morning and afternoon "tea fix" at their desks! Prepared in a metal teapot, taken straight off the fire, it is brewed by boiling water and milk with tea leaves and sugar, hence called doodhpati (milk and tea leaves). And for most of us, the general consensus is that a cup of good tea makes everything better!

6 to 8 servings

- **8 cups of boiling water**
- **8 tsp of black tea leaf or 8 tea bags, without strings or pins**
- **Pinch of sugar**
- **8 leaves of fresh mint**
- **4 small strands of lemon grass**
- **½ cup milk**

Rinse the teapot with hot water and add the tea, sugar, mint and lemongrass. Pour boiling water over it. Cover and steep for 5 to 8 minutes. Give the pot a stir and add the milk.

Serve hot with additional sugar and milk to top up as preferred.

Tips

- Water has to be boiling hot when poured over the tea. It cannot be tepid.
- Loose tea is the best. If you cannot access it use the strongest black tea bags available.
- Ensure that pins, strings or labels are unattached; these change the taste of the tea.
- Mint and lemon grass make for a perfect combination, adding delicate flavour to the tea.

Batasa and Choi
Tea and Batasa

Batasa — Parsi Butter Biscuit

Batasas are simple teatime biscuits with a long history and a wonderful legendary story. As the Dutch colonisers left the shores of the Indian port city of Surat in the 1700s, a flourishing bakery was handed over to a local employee Faramji Dotivala. This baker continued to produce the breads for the local British — the next set of colonisers.

Once the Brits too lessened in numbers, the breads' popularity diminished and the wasted bread was soon distributed to the local poor. Having the advantage of being fermented with an ingredient called Toddy, there was little chance of the bread ever catching fungus, prolonging the life of this staple yet making it harder in texture and more difficult to eat.

Local doctors also started suggesting that this stale bread be given as a convalescent food to patients as it was easy to digest and kept their stomachs feeling full for long. Dotivala started producing smaller specially dried bread buns for this purpose, and hence created 'batasas' which were produced using the same 3 ingredients of toddy, flour and water! They were round balls of dough, baked and to be eaten with a cup of sweet tea. They were hard enough to be dunked into the tea and not fall apart.

Years later, the Batasa was changed to a richer version with an addition of butter and or ghee (clarified butter). With alcohol prohibition taking place soon after, Toddy was replaced with yeast or even completely omitted in the recipe.

Besides the cities of Surat, Navsari and Pune where Batasas are rivalled to be called their own, it was and still is a staple sold in Irani Tea Houses in Mumbai and until recently even in Karachi. Sadly, these cafes are dwindling down in numbers. With a strong sense of revival of Parsi food, many of us hope to soon walk through the doors of the first wonderful Irani Tea House in the West!

Today, Batasas are still made from only a few ingredients, and can be crisp or flaky. There is even an amazing cheese batasa, popular among the Parsis of Canada. Adding cumin or caraway seeds, toasted slivered almonds are more traditional options. I like mine plain and simple.

The shape continues to be mainly round like the original buns!

Makes 60 Batasas

- **4 cups sifted flour**
- **1 tbsp semolina**
- **3 tsp baking powder**
- **1 1/2 tsp salt**
- **226 gm/8 oz soft butter,cut into pieces**
- **8 tbsp cold water**

- **Optional ingredients:**
- 2 oz toasted slivered peeled almonds
- 1 tsp cardamom powder
- 2 tsp caraway or cumin seeds
- ½ cup hard strong cheddar while beating the butter

In a bowl mix the dry ingredients. Add the softened butter in little pieces. With the tip of your fingers crumble the mixture until it resembles little beads. Add any options now. You can alternately use two butter knives or place all of it in a food processor using the pulse button.

Add the cold water 1 tablespoon at a time until it all comes together. Do not over knead.

Roll out into a long even sausage on a lightly dusted floured surface. Cut this into 48-60 even pieces. Roll each one very lightly into a ball.

Place on a baking sheet.

Preheat the oven to 325 F/165 C. Cook the batasas for 30 minutes. Then lower the temperature to 275 F/135 C and cook for another 30 minutes.

Then lower the oven temperature to 225 F/105 C and cook for another hour or so, until dried from the inside.

Leave to cool and store in an airtight box.

Tips

- If you have a cake beater use the 'k beater' attachment to mix. If you have a food processor it will take less than 5 minutes to put this together. Overturn all of it on to a cutting board, cut into 2 or 4 equal pieces and work with one at a time. It is much quicker and will help make each one evenly.
- Keep the baking trays ready with grease proof paper or grease the tray lightly with butter. You will need two large cookie sheets to fit all of them.
- The trick is to dry the batasas from the inside and so the heat variation is very important.
- Batasas should have a light pinky colour and not be white.
- Try to keep them all even in size which helps bake them at the same time.

Kumas, a saffron
and almond cake

Kumas — Teatime Parsi Cake

Kumas is a Parsi cake that has Persian roots. Made up of semolina, saffron and almonds it gets its moistness from yogurt. It is dense and simply delicious. Flavoured with cardamom and nutmeg and made with a combination of whole and wheat flours gives the Kumas its uniqueness.

This is my mum's version, highly perfected. I proudly share it today with all of you since I have yet to eat a better Kumas anywhere in the world. She has been requested to bake this for weddings, baby showers, Navroze, tea parties and more. Everyone talks about it amongst her family and friends. Try it out for yourself.

Eating it with a dollop of fresh clotted cream makes it even more heavenly and it can even be eaten with a slice of good cheddar cheese if you prefer.

Makes 24 square pieces

Prepare a deep 13x9 inch/33x22cm rectangle or 25 cm/10 inch round cake tin with butter and flour.

- 170 gm/6 oz salted butter at room temperature
- 2-cups sugar
- 5 eggs
- 1-cup wheat flour
- 1-cup semolina
- ¾ cup plain flour

- 2 tsp baking powder
- 1 tsp salt
- 4 tsp ground cardamom powder
- 3 tsp grated nutmeg
- 1 ½ cup yogurt, which has been left out of the fridge for 24 hours

Step 1:

In a bowl sift together, the wheat semolina, plain flour, baking powder, salt, the ground cardamom and freshly scraped nutmeg powder.

Step 2:

In a cup, mix together1 ½ cup yogurt with 2 tsp crushed saffron.

It should be sour and not fresh.

Step 3:

In a cake mixer, place the cake beater attachment and cream the butter and sugar.

Add the 5 eggs one at a time. Reduce the speed to a gentle stir, adding one third of the dry mix and half of the yogurt, repeat and finish it off with the flour. Allow it to stir until smooth.

Add and fold in with a spatula,

¾ cup chopped almonds – keep some of it aside for the top.

Pour this mixture into the prepared pan. Sprinkle with the chopped almonds. Bake in a pre-heated oven of 180 C/350 F for up to 1 hour or until the toothpick comes out clear when tested. Do not overbake as it will be dry.

Tips

- Saffron is best kept in the refrigerator and can be easily crushed with the back of the spoon as it gets crisp which is an easier method. Alternately, you could boil the strands of saffron in a little warm water and then add it to the cake.
- If you don't have time to sour the yogurt, use ¾ cup buttermilk and ¾ cup yogurt to create the sourness.
- The "watery" part of the yogurt is great for this recipe; do not discard it.
- Remember to sift both the flours. It helps make the cake lighter and fluffier and is a very necessary step.
- Use coarse semolina and not the fine variety preferably.
- Almonds are with skin and whole. Roughly chop this leaving the larger pieces aside for the topping as in the picture.
- If you are using a round cake pan, cooking time may be an extra 10-15 minutes, as the pan could be deeper than the rectangle one.

Khatai
Parsi Sweet Cookies

Khatai Biscuits

A mix of Persian and Indian origins this sweet biscuit has a charm of its own. There are a few variations of this treat, which stem from its places of origin, often using a variety of flour, semolina, rice flour, wheat flour but all made with ghee or clarified butter.

As regions separated and parted ways from their Empire, so did the biscuits!

Persians make these with rice flour or chickpea flour and call it Nan-e-Berenji. They flavour their delights with rosewater and dried crushed rose petals. They also tend to use poppy seeds to dot them. Their biscuit is smoother in texture and melts in the mouth.

However, Indians make these with a mix of semolina and plain flour and call it Nan-Khatai, originally from Surat in Gujarat and hence a part of the Parsi food repertoire. Using cardamom and nutmeg powders to flavour it and topping it with an almond or cashew nut and crossed with an X, stamps it as our own!

As the Zoroastrians moved inland to Navsari and Pune they took their fine food culture with them. It now tends to be a healthy competition of which of the three cities produces the best teatime snacks! The Chai-Khana or the Irani tea-house (Irani Cafés) were ever so popular in the Indian Sub-continent for decades. A reasonably priced meeting place, for the locals of the area and very often treated as a free "Club" for many, being there was an opportunity to enjoy a cup of tea with a savoury or sweet treat, day or night.

As Parsi – Zoroastrian migration to the West continues to occur significantly and in large numbers, it seems cultural traditions yearn for starting up a Chai-Khana too. Somehow I can already picture a modern day café offering Wi-Fi and yet retaining an old world charm with all the scrumptious treats to be savoured – perhaps a simple teahouse helping to link old cultures with new ones, a delightful reminder of an era gone by.

Makes 24 Khatai Biscuits

- **237gm/8 oz soft butter (see tips)**
- **237 gm/8 oz sugar**
- **2 ½ cups plain flour**
- **3 tbsp semolina**
- **Pinch of salt**
- **2 tsp cardamom**
- **1 tsp nutmeg**

In a cake mixer, gently beat until fluffy, the butter and sugar.

Add in and mix to form a large ball; plain flour, semolina, salt, cardamom and nutmeg.

Make 24 small balls, flatten to small disc and place on a greased or parchment-lined baking sheet. Cut an X mark lightly on each one. Put 4 slivers of almonds on each quarter, pressing it in firmly but gently.

Bake in an oven of 350 F/175 C degrees for 15-20 minutes.

Cool completely and store in an airtight container.

- If the mixture is dry, add a spoonful of milk or yogurt.
- Ghee, clarified butter, is a wonderful option to add for a crispy yet tasty nan khatai. I like to make it with ¼ ghee and ¾ butter whenever I can. You can also try half butter half ghee if you prefer.
- The Khatai should be pinky in colour, but it always darkens a little more from the bottom.
- The softness will depend on how much you flatten each disc of ball. The flatter you press the crispier it will be. The flatter you keep it the softer and chewier it turns out.
- Leave it to rest for 30 minutes before baking if you have the time.
- They freeze beautifully before baking. I prepare them in batches and bake straight from frozen whenever desired. Use sheets of parchment paper to keep them separated.

Chaapat
Parsi Pancakes

Chaapat – Parsi Sweet Pancakes

Pronounced as Cha- putt, simply meaning 'flat', these pancakes are an easy and quick teatime treat. They are an old favourite from the yesteryears, made from a mixture of coconut milk, nuts and a little sugar to enjoy with a cup of tea.

As in most traditional foods, each family has their secret recipe. This one is shared from my mother-in-law's family, which had a reputation for being great cooks in the Parsi community!

I have tweaked the ingredients, substituting regional or traditional ones with more readily available ones. But, they are still a delicious delight!

6 to 8 servings

- **2 cups coconut milk, from a box or tin**
- **200 gm/7 oz plain flour**
- **200 gm/7 oz sugar**
- **4 eggs**
- **½ tbsp melted ghee or clarified butter**
- **30 gm/1 oz almonds, blanched and grated**

- **15 gm/ ½ oz chopped pistachios**
- **30 gm/1 oz chopped charoli**
- **1 tsp vanilla essence**
- **½ tsp cardamom powder**
- **¼ tsp freshly scraped nutmeg**
- **½ tsp saffron threads, crushed**

Mix together with an electric hand beater until it all comes together, the coconut milk, flour, sugar, eggs, ghee, almonds, pistachios, charoli, vanilla, cardamom, nutmeg and saffron. Its consistency will be similar to pancake batter.

Heat a small 13cm/5" skillet. Place a drop of ghee and pour a ladle of the mixture. Tilt the pan in circles so the mixture spreads around evenly covering the bottom base of the pan.

Lower the heat and allow it to cook for a minute until a pale golden brown. Carefully flip it over and cook for another minute. Repeat until all are made.

Serve immediately or gently warm.

Tips

- The nuts chosen here are sweet but you can substitute with your favourite ones.
- The original recipe does call for Charoli, commonly found in India and in their larger Indian stores across the world; Macadamia nuts are the closest to these ones.
- Crush the saffron threads to help blend into the mixture. If you store the box of saffron in the fridge, it will crisp up and make it easier to crush. Use the tips of your fingers!

- If you do not wish to buy ghee, clarified brown butter is just as good. Simply melt and boil ½ cup of butter until it separates and changes its colour. Cool and use as needed.
- If the mixture becomes thick, add some milk to bring it to the right consistency. If it is thinner, refrigerate and wait for an hour or two for it to thicken, as the gluten in the flour will help do just that.
- Chaapats are only slightly sweetened and not overly sugary.

Malido and Papri

Malido

Traditionally served as part of the prayers for the family passed on, the Malido and Papdi is an integral part of the tray of food offered for to pray upon. It was the presiding priest and his wife that made this often tedious but delicious Parsi sweet dish. Then there was the rich version of it, with lots of pistachios and almonds added, and many more steps to get there.

Not generally eaten on birthdays and happy celebrations, the Malido is no longer a part of our younger generations' must-eat list. But as everything evolves, the Zoroastrians in the West have come up with an easy yet authentic-tasting Malido for everyone to have easy access to and carry on with tradition. I got this recipe from an elderly aunt, who does not recall who actually shared this with her, but I have tweaked it ever so slightly and am now sharing it with you to enjoy.

The Papdi, a hard flat-bread that completes the dish is difficult to make but available to buy. Interestingly on one of my travels to Spain, sitting at the breakfast buffet I noticed something very similar to the papdi – a Torta de Aceite, and it is perfect. A happy find, I brought back a few to share. A few months later, our local supermarket managed to import it and another bakery replicates it locally. I have been sharing this with others since the past 5 years and I do know you can find the same in the UK and some places in Canada and in the USA.

6 to 8 servings

- 57 gm/2 oz canola oil
- 57 gm/2 oz butter
- 1-cup coarse semolina
- ½ cup Bisquick
- 1 ½ cups sugar
- 1 ½ cups of water

- 2 tsp vanilla essence
- 3 tbsp rosewater
- 1 tsp freshly ground cardamom
- 1 tsp freshly ground nutmeg
- Pinch of salt

- For The Garnish
- 57 gm/2 oz slivered almonds

- 28 gm/1 oz slivered raisins
- 1 tbsp oil

Step 1 – The base

In a pot, heat the oil and butter over low heat. Add the semolina and cook for 5 to 10 minutes, until golden brown. Stir constantly. Add to this the Bisquick and continue cooking for another few minutes until combined.

Step 2 – Caramel Syrup or Aik Taar no seero

In a large pot, on medium heat, add 2 tbsp of the total sugar; melt completely and until golden caramel brown in colour.

Lower the heat and quickly pour cold water. Stir until melted. Do not let it boil at this point. Add the rest of the sugar and dissolve completely. The heat should be off or on very low. Once every grain of sugar is melted bring the mixture to a boil and make it a one-thread syrup or "aik taar no seero".

Remove from the heat and add the semolina and Bisquick mixture to it, stirring until smooth. Add vanilla essence, rosewater, cardamom and nutmeg.

Now return to a low heat and cook for 3-5 minutes, allowing the mixture to bubble.

Serve with fried slivered almonds and raisins.

Tips

- Aik taar no seero (one thread syrup) is best described as a liquid caramel. To test, dip a wooden spoon in the liquid mixture. Hold the spoon pointing downward. When the last bit of liquid drips off, it should form one teardrop. Do it often once the caramel is boiling and as it thickens the drop will become clearer and more apparent. It is the perfect way to know when it is done. If two teardrops fall clearly it is thicker but is then called bey taar no seero (two thread syrup)!
- The semolina should be as coarse as you can find it for a good texture.
- When you add the Bisquick the mixture will rise fast and furious so ensure your pan is large enough and it does not spill over. It will then all settle down. This is because there is soda bicarbonate in the Bisquick.
- Use a whisk to mix and stir. This will work efficiently and quickly to keep the lumps away.
- The rosewater is light and flowery, it is not the same as an essence. It is available in Indian, Persian and Middle Eastern Stores and in many of the International food aisles of supermarkets.
- Malido is best served warm and can be kept refrigerated for a week.

Parsi Cook's Spice Island

103. Garam Masala

103. About Dhansak Masala

106. The Ancient Art of Grinding Spices

109. Traditional Ingredients for Curry Masala Paste (the picture)

Garam Masala; cinnamon, cardamom, black peppercorns and cloves

Garam Masala – A blend of spices

Garam Masala is most versatile. It can be strong and pungent or aromatic and flavourful.

I vote for the latter. This is my mum's recipe, which I personally enjoy cooking with, and I am not the only one! There are the die-hard fans, which to this day request her to grind it for them whenever they get a chance. For best results, dry grind it in a coffee grinder or any other dry food grinder. The Garam Masala can be stored in a glass jar for up to 1 year.

- **3 cinnamon sticks – about 3 tbsp once ground into a powder**
- **1 ½ tbsp peeled cardamom pods (without the green skin)**
- **¾ tbsp black peppercorns**
- **¾ tbsp cloves**

In a coffee grinder, grind all ingredients together until it is a fine powder. Fill a dry glass jar and store.

About Dhansak Masala

The Dhansak Masala is available in most Indian Stores worldwide under the same label. Each one may be prepared with a slight variation. I continue to use the same one from the Empress Market in Karachi where I grew up!

Dhansak Masala; cumin, coriander, cardamom, cloves, mace, nutmeg, cinnamon, turmeric, saffron, fenugreek, dry red chillies and bay leaves.

Mortar and Pestle

Masala no Pathar

Photo Courtesy Raizan Mavalvala

The Ancient Art of Grinding Spices

Technology and state-of-the-art machinery has helped ease our lives inside and outside the kitchen. However, the methods of centuries past, in preparing key ingredients for our food, had benefits in their own right: for instance, the ancient art of grinding daily 'masala'. In most homes in the subcontinent, many had, and many still have, indigenous stone grinders. The "Spice Stone" or "Masala no Pathar", as we refer to it in Gujarati, was generally made from limestone, containing calcium. This gave the family an added health benefit of calcium, as it was combined with the masalas and dissolved into the food, therefore entering their daily diet.

Besides the sub-continental countries such as Pakistan, India, Bangladesh, Nepal, and Sri Lanka, it is well known that the Indonesians, Malaysians and Singaporeans continue using their versions of traditional Masala stones.

Having grown up watching the grinding of masalas on a stone when I was a little girl, I have a vivid memory of the process. To start off, the stone would be washed in warm water and any excess water would be removed with one's bare hands. Salt would be sprinkled and then all the ingredients for that day's masala were laid out on the stone. Masalas were primarily made up of hard coconut flesh, ginger, garlic, a variety of dry and fresh chilies – these were ground together and turned into a beautiful thick paste.

Generally, all the larger pieces were smashed together with the side of the pestle and brought together; then rolled over with the heavy pin again and again. It would need some liquid to form a paste, the same principle of using the grinder, and so warm water kept in a bowl on the side was added. Vinegar and tamarind juice, an integral part of the recipe in any Parsi cooking, were also often used. Great care was taken to wash the stone well, as the acidic ingredients affected the limestone.

I went to a traditional all-girls school in Karachi, where cooking classes were part of our curriculum, and we got the chance to make use of this wonderful tradition. In fact, it was frowned upon to use an electric blender to prepare your curry masalas, as everyone who actually mastered the art of using the stones continued to promise us a very special flavour and consistency. I would be questioning this statement if I had not had a chance to experience this first hand. But the smoothness and silky feel between your fingers is unlike anything we can see using modern day marvels.

These slabs of limestone are cut into a rectangular shape, large and small, in preparation to be sold. It is a two-piece set with the second piece being a small rectangle pestle much like a rolling pin but flatter. Generally those were hand-picked by the person using it, ensuring the rolling pin is comfortable to use and not too heavy nor too light – much like a chef's personalised knife.

The stone dresser would take chisels and make small depressions all over the stone in preparation for it to be used. This would prevent the coconut, chillies, onions, ginger, garlic and other ingredients, from slipping and sliding all over the place. Most homes also kept a pestle and mortar to crush seeds and peppers.

Though I am far from ever wishing a revisit to this laborious process, and I am eternally grateful for all the modern day gadgetry invented, the history of the Masala no Pathar is an integral part of the story of our ancient Parsi cuisine.

Tips

- If anyone being adventurous enough should decide to go ahead and try grinding their spices on a stone, please make sure to wash your hands thoroughly with soap and water so as not to get the sting in your eyes!

Traditional Ingredients for
Curry Masala Paste